BE
DONE
WITH
IT

ALSO BY ROBERT T. YARBOROUGH

Beyond Space and Time

Getting Down to Brass Tacks

The Outrage Paradox

The Self Coaching Blueprint

Quantum Whispers

BE DONE WITH IT

Let Go of the Past, Embrace the Present, and Live Unburdened

Robert T. Yarborough

Pranava Books

Publisher's Cataloging-in-Publication Data
Yarborough, Robert T., 1960–
Be Done With It: Let Go of the Past, Embrace the Present, and Live Unburdened / Robert T. Yarborough.
— First edition.
p. cm.
ISBN: 979-8-9912582-1-0
    1.Self-help. 2. Mindfulness (Psychology). 3. Surrender (Psychology). 4. Personal growth. 5. Letting go (Psychology). I. Title.
BF637.S4 Y37 2025
    158.1 — dc23
LCCN: 2025901623

Printed in the United States of America
10 9 8 7 6 5 4 3 2 1

Dedication

To my incredible children,

You are my greatest teachers. In your laughter, I have learned the beauty of presence.

This book is for you—not as a lesson, but as a reminder: Life is not something to be conquered or controlled. It is something to be lived with openness, trust, and joy. May you always walk lightly, embrace change, and discover the freedom of being unburdened.

With all my love,

Dad

Table of Contents

A Fellow Traveler on the Journey

"Letting go gives us freedom, and freedom is the only condition for happiness. If, in our heart, we still cling to anything—anger, anxiety, or possessions—we cannot be free."

— Thích Nhat Hanh

I am not a spiritual teacher, a guru, or a leader. I do not claim to hold all the answers or to have reached some final state of enlightenment. Like you, I am simply someone navigating the complexities of life—its joys, challenges, and mysteries. This book does not come from a place of authority but from a place of exploration. It reflects my journey in learning to let go, live fully, and embrace the freedom that arises when we are truly *done* with the things that no longer serve us.

The ideas within these pages were not born out of mastery but out of practice. There have been moments in my life when I clung tightly—to fear, resentment, expectations, and the need for control—only to realize that holding on was the very source of my suffering. I have also experienced the peace and liberation that come when I let go, even briefly, and allow life to unfold as it will. It is from these moments of clarity, as well as the struggles in between, that this book emerged.

I wrote this not as a teacher speaking to a student but as a fellow traveler walking beside you. We all take the journey of letting go in our own way, and it is never complete. Every day offers new opportunities to release what weighs us down, trust life's unfolding, and reconnect with the present moment. I hope these words will resonate with you, not as instructions but as invitations to pause, reflect, and discover what letting go might mean for you.

Why This Book Exists

This book exists because I needed it myself. I needed to explore what it means to live without clinging, to let go of the past, to stop fearing the future, and to trust the present moment. I needed to remind myself that freedom is not something we achieve through effort but something we uncover through surrender. If these reflections resonate with you, it is because they come from a shared human experience— the struggle to find peace in a world that often feels chaotic and uncertain.

You may not agree with every idea in this book, which is okay. I intend not to prescribe a single path but to spark curiosity and inspire exploration. If even one sentence here opens a door within you, inviting you to experience life more freely, then this book has served its purpose.

Being Done

The title of this book, *Be Done With It*, is not about giving up on life or disengaging from the world. It is about releasing the things that no longer serve us: the resistance, the fear, the need to control, and the weight of the past. It is about being done with the patterns of thought and behavior that keep us trapped in cycles of suffering. It is about stepping into the freedom of living unburdened, fully present, and deeply connected to life as it is.

Being done does not mean being perfect, nor does it mean you will never feel fear, resistance, or attachment again. It simply means recognizing these patterns when they arise and choosing, moment by moment, to let them go. It is a practice, not a destination—a journey, not an endpoint.

An Invitation

As you read this book, I invite you to approach it with an open heart and mind. Let these words be a mirror, reflecting your own experiences and insights. Take what resonates, leave what doesn't, and trust your inner wisdom to guide you.

You are not alone on this journey. I am walking it too, as are countless others who, like us, are learning to release what no longer serves and embrace the freedom of the now. Together, we are discovering what it means to be done—not with life, but with the illusions that keep us from fully living it.

Thank you for allowing me to share this journey with you. May this book be a companion on your path, reminding you of the peace, joy, and freedom already within you, waiting to be rediscovered.

With gratitude...
—Robert T. Yarborough
January 2025

A Journey Into Freedom

"To let go does not mean to get rid of. To let go means to let be. When we let be with compassion, things come and go on their own."

— Jack Kornfield

This book is not a set of instructions or a manual for self-improvement. It is an invitation. An invitation to step beyond the noise of the mind and into the stillness of your being. An invitation to recognize that the freedom you seek is not found in striving or controlling but in letting go. It is not something you achieve but uncover—a truth that has always been within you, waiting to be seen.

Life, as most of us live it, feels heavy. We carry the weight of the past, the anxiety of the future, and the relentless chatter of the mind. This weight creates a sense of disconnection from ourselves, others, and the present moment. But this disconnection is not reality; it is an illusion. And like all illusions, it dissolves the moment you see through it.

This book is about how we resist life, cling to what no longer serves us, and create suffering by trying to control what is beyond our control. It is about recognizing the patterns of the mind and stepping into the spaciousness of awareness, where freedom is not something to be sought but something to be realized.

Letting Go Is Liberation

The central message of this book is simple: Letting go is not about loss but liberation. It is about releasing the resistance, attachments, and fears that keep you trapped in cycles of suffering. Letting go is not an act of giving up—it is an act of opening up. It is a way of aligning yourself with the flow of life, trusting its unfolding, and discovering the peace that comes from living in harmony with what is.

When you let go, you do not lose yourself. On the contrary, you rediscover yourself. You reconnect with the part of you that is beyond thought, beyond identity, beyond the stories the mind tells. This part of you—your true self—is always present, always whole, and always free. The process of letting go is simply a process of remembering this truth.

The Three Movements of Freedom

This book is divided into three parts, each exploring a movement toward freedom:

Part One: The Weight of Holding On. Here, we explore the burdens we carry—the attachments, fears, and resistance that keep us tethered to the past and anxious about the future. We look at how these patterns arise and how they create suffering.

Part Two: Living in the Now. In this section, we dive into the power of presence. We examine what living fully in the now means, free from the mind's chatter and the ego's need for control. Practical practices like mindfulness and self-awareness help anchor you in this space of presence.

Part Three: Moving Beyond. Finally, we explore what it means to let go. From surrender and acceptance to embracing the unknown, this part of the book invites you to step into the freedom of living unburdened. Here, you discover the beauty of impermanence and the joy of trusting life's unfolding.

Each chapter builds on the last, offering philosophical reflections and practical steps to deepen your understanding and integrate these truths into your life.

An Invitation to Awareness

This book is not about changing who you are; it is about uncovering who you already are. It is about noticing the patterns of the mind, not to judge them, but to step beyond them. It is about creating space—space between you and your thoughts, space for awareness to arise, and space for freedom to emerge.

As you read, approach these pages with curiosity and openness. This is not a book to be rushed through or analyzed; it is a book to be felt, experienced, and reflected upon. Let the words guide you back to the stillness within yourself. Let the reflections lead you to your own insights. And let the practices help you reconnect with the freedom that is always available, right here, in the now.

The Journey Ahead

This is a journey without a map because the destination is not somewhere out there—it is already here. You are not being asked to strive, achieve, or become. You are simply being asked to let go. Let go of the weight you have been carrying. Let go of the need to control. Let go of the fear that keeps you clinging to what no longer serves you. In this letting go, you will find not emptiness but fullness. Not loss, but liberation.

The mind will resist this message, as it resists anything it cannot grasp or control. But trust that something deeper in you already knows the truth of these words. Trust that the freedom you seek is not far away—it is within you, waiting to be realized.

So, let us begin this journey not by adding something new to your life but by removing what does not belong. Let us step beyond the illusions of the mind and into the freedom of the now. And in this freedom, may you find the peace, joy, and wholeness that have always been yours.

Chapter One

The Burden of the Past

"People have a hard time letting go of their suffering. Out of a fear of the unknown, they prefer suffering that is familiar."

— Thích Nhat Hanh

The past is like a shadow, always following you but never truly present. It exists only in the mind as a collection of memories that we replay over and over again, convincing ourselves that they are still relevant. These memories—whether of joy, pain, or regret—become the filters through which we see our lives. And because of this, they bind us to suffering.

Think of how often your thoughts drift to the past. A conversation you wish had gone differently. A mistake you feel you should never have made. A relationship that ended too soon, or one that lasted too long. These fragments of memory become like emotional weights that you carry everywhere you go, sapping your energy and clouding your perception of the present moment.

But here's the truth: the past is gone. It has no life of its own. It can only exist if you keep it alive in your mind.

Memories as Mental Constructs

Memories, by their very nature, are not reliable. They are not faithful recordings of reality but subjective interpretations filtered through your emotions, beliefs, and perspectives. What you remember is not the event itself but your experience of it—colored by your state of mind at the time and further distorted by the passing of time. And yet, we cling to these memories as if they hold the ultimate truth about who we are and what life is.

When you identify with your memories, you begin to weave a story about yourself: *This is what happened to me, and this is why I am the way I am* This story may provide a sense of identity but also traps you in a cycle of reliving the same emotions and experiences. The pain of the past becomes your pain in the present, not because it is still happening, but because you are keeping it alive.

Grievances and the Need to Be Right

Grievances are a hefty burden. They arise when we feel wronged or betrayed, and they thrive on our need to be right. We replay the offense in our minds, reinforcing the narrative of victimhood: *They shouldn't have done that to me,* or *I deserve an apology* Each time we replay the grievance, we strengthen our attachment to it, as though holding onto it will somehow make things right.

But grievances are not about justice. They are about the ego's need to preserve itself. The ego thrives on conflict and separation. It convinces you that letting go of a grievance would mean admitting defeat or condoning the wrong. In reality, holding onto grievances only deepens your suffering. The person who wronged you may have long moved on, but you remain imprisoned by your anger and resentment.

Letting go of grievances is not about excusing what happened. It is about freeing yourself from the emotional chains that bind you to the past. It is recognizing that the only one suffering from your anger is you.

Regrets and the Illusion of Control

Regrets are another way the past binds us to suffering. They stem from the belief that we could have changed the outcome if we had acted differently. This belief is rooted in the illusion of control—that we have the power to rewrite the past if only we think about it long enough.

Unfortunately, no amount of regret can alter what has already happened. The past is fixed, unchangeable, and beyond your reach. Clinging to regret is like staring at a closed door, hoping it will magically reopen. Meanwhile, life unfolds around you, but you cannot see it because you are fixated on what is already gone.

Regret is a thief of the present moment. It keeps you locked in a cycle of self-blame, distracting you from the opportunities and possibilities of now. To release regret is to accept that the past cannot be undone but that the future is shaped by the choices you make in this moment.

The Self-Perpetuating Cycle of Suffering

What makes the burden of the past so heavy is that it feeds on itself. The more you dwell on memories, grievances, and regrets, the stronger their hold on you becomes. They generate emotions—anger, sadness, guilt—that reinforce the mental patterns keeping you stuck. These emotions then influence your thoughts and actions, creating a cycle of suffering that feels impossible to break.

The key to breaking this cycle is awareness. When you become aware of the mental and emotional patterns that bind you to the past, you create a space between yourself and the burden you are carrying. In that space, you can see that the burden is not who you are. It is something you are holding onto—but you have the power to set it down.

Freedom from the Past

The past has no power over you except the power you give it. When you recognize this, you begin to see that the burden of the past is optional. You do not have to carry it. You can choose to let it go.

Letting go of the past does not mean denying its existence or its impact on your life. It means acknowledging it fully and then releasing it, understanding that it no longer defines you. You are not your memories, grievances, or regrets. You are the awareness in which these experiences arise and fade away.

The question is not, "How can I change the past?" but, "Am I willing to release my attachment to it?" When the answer is yes, you step into a freedom beyond the grasp of memory, a freedom always available to you in the present moment.

How Identifying with the "Story of Me" Creates a False Sense of Self

We all carry a narrative—a collection of memories, experiences, beliefs, and labels that we use to define who we are. This narrative is what Eckhart Tolle[1] calls the "story of me." It is the mental construct we create to give our lives

---

[1] Eckhart Tolle, A New Earth: Awakening to Your Life's Purpose (New York: Penguin Group, 2005).

coherence and meaning. At first glance, this seems harmless, even necessary. After all, who are we without our stories? But this identification with the "story of me" creates a false sense of self that binds us to suffering and keeps us disconnected from the truth of who we are.

The Nature of the Story

The "story of me" is not a reflection of your true self but a patchwork of past experiences and external influences. It includes:

Memories: Events you've lived through, both joyful and painful.

Labels: The roles you identify with—parent, professional, victim, success, failure.

Beliefs: Ideas about who you are and what you are capable of, often shaped by others.

Grievances: The wounds you've carried, the injustices you've suffered.

Accomplishments: The things you've done that validate your sense of worth.

While these elements feel deeply personal, they are not the essence of who you are. They are mental constructs—stories your mind tells to give you a sense of identity. The problem arises when you begin to mistake the story for the self.

The Illusion of Permanence

The "story of me" feels solid, permanent, and unchanging, but in truth, it is fluid and ever-evolving. Think back to who you believed yourself to be ten years ago. How much of that identity still holds true today? Likely, many aspects of your story have shifted—relationships have changed, beliefs have evolved, and roles have come and gone. And yet, despite this impermanence, the mind clings to the story, believing it to be the fixed essence of who you are.

This illusion of permanence creates a false sense of self—a self that is fragile, vulnerable, and constantly seeking validation to reinforce its existence. When the story is challenged—when life doesn't align with your constructed narrative—you feel threatened, as though your very existence is at stake.

Attachment to the Story

The deeper your attachment to the "story of me," the more it limits you. You become defined by your past, what has happened to you, and how others perceive you. This attachment creates a sense of separateness, as though you are a distinct entity navigating a world of "others." It reinforces the ego's need to compare, judge, and defend itself, perpetuating a cycle of conflict and suffering.

For instance:

> If your story is one of victimhood, you may unconsciously seek situations that confirm this narrative, even when they no longer serve you.

> If your story is one of success, you may fear failure to such an extent that you avoid taking risks or embracing change.

> If your story is tied to a specific identity—such as a job title or role—you may feel lost or unmoored when life inevitably shifts, and that identity no longer applies.

In each case, the story limits your ability to respond to life authentically, keeping you stuck in patterns that no longer align with the present moment.

The False Self vs. the True Self

The "story of me" is the ego's creation—a mental construct that relies on external validation and comparison to maintain its sense of existence. It is a mask, a role you play, but it is not the truth of who you are.

Your true self, in contrast, is not tied to any story. It is the awareness beneath the narrative—the still, silent presence that observes your thoughts, emotions, and experiences without becoming entangled in them. This awareness is timeless, unchanging, and whole. It does not need a story to validate its existence.

When you identify with the "story of me," you obscure your connection to this deeper self. You become so enmeshed in the narrative that you lose sight of the awareness that holds it all.

Letting Go of the Story

To free yourself from the false self, you must first recognize the "story of me" for what it is: a mental construct, not a reflection of reality. This requires cultivating awareness and questioning the narrative you've been telling yourself:

Is this story true, or is it just my interpretation?

Does this story serve me, or does it limit me?

Who am I beyond this story?

As you begin to let go of the story, you create space for something deeper to emerge. This is not about erasing your past or denying your experiences. It is about seeing them as part of a larger flow of life rather than as defining elements of who you are.

In letting go of the story, you reconnect with your true self—the always present awareness, free from labels, roles, and attachments. You realize that you are not the story but the space in which the story unfolds. This shift in perspective is profoundly liberating. It allows you to engage with life fully without being bound by the weight of the past or the need to construct a specific future.

Living Beyond the Story

Living beyond the "story of me" means embracing life as it is, moment by moment, without the filter of past narratives. It means seeing yourself not as a fixed identity but as a dynamic, evolving being intimately connected to the flow of existence.

When you release the false self, you find that life becomes lighter, freer, and more authentic. You no longer feel the need to defend your story or cling to it for a sense of worth. Instead, you rest in the peace of knowing that who *you* are cannot be defined by any narrative—it is far greater, far deeper, and far more expansive than the mind could ever conceive.

The Burden of the Past and the Illusion of Time

Our relationship to the past is deeply tied to the concept of time—a framework the mind relies on to make sense of life. We see time as linear, divided into past, present, and future. This perception shapes our experiences, but it is, at its core, an illusion. The past exists only in the mind as memory, and the future exists only as imagination. The only reality is the present moment.

The past holds power over us only because the mind believes it can—or must—rewrite it. This belief arises from the illusion of control, the idea that we can dictate how life unfolds or repair what has already happened. But clinging to this illusion is like trying to grip sand in your hands—the tighter you hold on, the more it slips away. This illusion of time perpetuates suffering, keeping us trapped in a cycle of reliving what is no longer real. To truly free ourselves from the burden of the past, we must first understand how the mind's need for control keeps us trapped

The Mind's Creation of Time

The mind is a powerful tool, but it is deeply conditioned to think in terms of time. It divides life into segments: what has happened, what is happening, and what will happen. This segmentation creates the illusion of continuity—a thread that ties together the events of our lives into a cohesive narrative.

When you recall a memory, where does it exist? It is not "out there" in the world, unfolding again. It exists only as a thought in your mind, triggered by an association or an emotion. The past is not a place you can revisit or change. It is a mental construct—a shadow cast by the mind onto the present moment.

The Past as a Mental Projection

The past feels real because of the emotional charge we attach to it. When we revisit a painful memory, we re-experience the associated emotions as though the event were happening again. This re-living keeps the past alive, not because it exists independently, but because we feed it with our attention.

The past is no more tangible than a dream. Just as a dream fades upon waking, the past dissolves when we stop revisiting it. The only thing that keeps it alive is the mind's habit of returning to it, over and over, like replaying a movie that has already ended.

The Weight of Illusory Time

The illusion of time amplifies the burden of the past by making it feel continuous and inescapable. We carry unresolved emotions, unfinished conversations, and unfulfilled expectations as though they were still active, as though we were still living in those moments. But the reality is that these moments are gone. The only place they exist is in our minds, and the only power they hold is the power we give them.

Each time we revisit the past, we drag it into the present, layering old experiences onto new ones. This creates a distortion, clouding our perception of reality by what we think should have been or could have been. The weight of these mental projections prevents us from fully engaging with the present moment, which is the only place where life is happening.

Freedom Through Presence

To free ourselves from the burden of the past, we must recognize time for what it is: an illusion. The past has no existence outside of the now. When we let go of the mental projection of time, we step into the present moment, where the past loses its grip on us.

Presence is the doorway to freedom. In the present moment, the mind does not need to revisit what has already passed. There is no room for regret, guilt, or grievance because those emotions require a time frame that does not exist in the now. The past dissolves when you bring your full attention to the present and, with it, the suffering it carries.

Practical Reflection: Observing Time as an Illusion

Notice Your Thoughts. Throughout the day, observe how often your thoughts drift to the past. Are you reliving a memory, replaying a conversation, or regretting an action? Each time you notice this, ask yourself: *Where is this event happening? Is it happening now, or is it only in my mind?*

Ground Yourself in the Present. When you catch yourself caught in the past, shift your attention to the present moment. Focus on your breath, the sensations in your body, or the sounds around you. Notice how the past fades when your awareness is fully rooted in now.

Question the Reality of the Past. Ask yourself: *Does this memory have power over me, or am I giving it power by revisiting it?* Recognize that the past exists only as a thought and that you have the choice to let it go.

The Past Is Not Who You Are

The greatest freedom comes from realizing that you are not your past. You are not the collection of memories, experiences, or labels your mind has constructed. You are the awareness in which all these things arise and dissolve. This awareness is timeless—it exists beyond the illusion of past and future.

When you release your attachment to the past, you reclaim the fullness of the present moment. You step into a space of clarity, peace, and possibility where the burdens of time no longer weigh you down. In this space, you discover that the freedom you seek has always been here, waiting for you to recognize it.

...

Chapter Two

The Illusion of Control

"You may not control all the events that happen to you, but you can decide not to be reduced by them."

— Maya Angelou

The desire for control is deeply embedded in the human experience. We believe that controlling our circumstances, people, and outcomes can create a life free from discomfort, unpredictability, and pain. Yet, this belief is an illusion. Control is a construct of the mind—a desperate attempt to impose order on the inherently uncertain flow of life. In clinging to this illusion, we create resistance, suffering, and a false sense of self.

To see through the illusion of control is recognizing the futility of trying to hold onto something constantly shifting and evolving. It is to surrender to the natural flow of life, not as a sign of defeat but as an act of profound liberation.

The Mind's Obsession with Control

The mind craves certainty and predictability. It seeks to map out the future, plan for every possible scenario, and ensure that life unfolds according to its expectations. This craving is rooted in fear—the fear of uncertainty, failure, loss, and, ultimately, not being in control.

But life is unpredictable by its very nature. No amount of planning or effort can guarantee a specific outcome. The more we try to control it, the more we resist its natural flow, and the more we suffer when it inevitably moves in unexpected ways.

Consider how often you try to control situations or people in your life. Do you attempt to dictate how others should behave, what they should think, or how they should feel? Do you replay events in your mind, imagining how you could have controlled the outcome? Do you resist change, clinging to what feels familiar and safe? Each of these tendencies is a symptom of the illusion of control.

Clinging to What Cannot Be Changed

The belief that we can change the unchangeable is at the heart of the illusion of control. We resist what is, wishing it were different. We replay the past, trying to rewrite it in our minds. We attempt to manipulate the future, hoping to bend it to our will. But life does not conform to the mind's expectations. It unfolds as it will, indifferent to our plans and desires.

This resistance to reality creates immense suffering. When we cling to what cannot be changed—be it the past, another person's behavior, or the inevitability of change itself—we expend our energy fighting a battle we cannot win. We remain stuck in a cycle of frustration, disappointment, and disconnection from the present moment.

The Ego's Need for Control

The illusion of control is closely tied to the ego. The ego believes that its survival depends on controlling the external world. It identifies with roles, possessions, and achievements, seeing them as extensions of itself. To the ego, losing control feels like losing its very identity.

The ego also clings to narratives about how life "should" be. It constructs rigid expectations and judges everything that falls short of these ideals. When reality does not align with the ego's expectations, it reacts with anger, frustration, or despair. In this way, the ego's need for control perpetuates suffering and keeps us trapped in a state of resistance.

The Futility of Control

No matter how much effort we put into controlling life, the truth remains: control is an illusion. Life is inherently dynamic, unpredictable, and beyond our grasp. Circumstances change, people evolve, and events unfold in ways we could never foresee. The more we cling to control, the more life reminds us of its impermanence.

Life cannot be contained or dictated. It can only be lived, moment by moment, with openness and acceptance.

Surrender as Liberation

Surrendering the illusion of control does not mean giving up or becoming passive. It means recognizing that while you cannot control life, you can choose how you respond to it. Surrender is an act of alignment with reality. It is the willingness to let go of resistance and flow with the current of life rather than against it.

Surrender is not defeat—it is freedom. When you let go of

the need to control, you release the weight of expectation and the fear of uncertainty. You begin to trust in life's natural intelligence, recognizing that it often unfolds in ways far greater than anything the mind could plan.

The Present Moment: The Only Place of True Power

The only place where you have any real influence is the present moment. You cannot control the past—it is gone. You cannot control the future—it has not yet arrived. But in this moment, you can choose to let go of resistance and meet life as it is.

When you live in the present moment, you see that control is unnecessary. Life unfolds perfectly, not because you dictate it, but because a deeper wisdom guides it. This wisdom is accessible to you when you release the illusion of control and rest in the stillness of now.

Reflection: Letting Go of Control

What in your life are you trying to control? Reflect on areas where you feel resistance or frustration. Are you clinging to a specific outcome, a person's behavior, or how life "should" be?

What would happen if you let go? Imagine releasing your need to control this situation. How might this change your experience? What emotions arise when you contemplate surrender?

Can you trust the flow of life? Consider moments in your life when things worked out in unexpected ways. What might this teach you about the wisdom of letting go?

Surrender is a Form of Strength, Not Weakness

The word *surrender* often carries negative connotations. It may evoke images of defeat, passivity, or giving up in the face of adversity. In a culture that values control, dominance, and perseverance, surrender is often misunderstood as a sign of weakness or failure. But true surrender is none of these things. It is an act of profound strength—a courageous choice to let go of resistance and align yourself with the natural flow of life.

Surrender requires more than passivity. It demands awareness, trust, and the willingness to release the ego's grip on what *should* be. To surrender is not to submit to life as a victim but to embrace it as a co-creator, open to the infinite possibilities that arise when you stop trying to control the uncontrollable.

The Courage of Surrender

Surrender is not for the faint of heart. It takes immense courage to release your need for control and accept life as it is. The ego clings tightly to its ideas of how things should be, fearing that letting go will leave it powerless or irrelevant. To surrender is to face this fear and step into the unknown, trusting that life will unfold as it should, even without your interference.

True strength lies not in resisting what is but in embracing it with grace. It is easy to fight against circumstances, cling to expectations, and insist that life conforms to your desires. But it takes great inner fortitude to release that resistance, stop struggling, and allow life to flow as it will.

The Strength to Let Go

Surrender is not about abandoning responsibility or disengaging from life. Rather, it is about recognizing where your true power lies: not in controlling external circumstances but in choosing how you respond to them. Letting go of resistance does not mean giving up—it means giving yourself permission to move beyond struggle and step into a space of greater clarity and peace.

Imagine holding onto a rope in a tug-of-war. The harder you pull, the more tension builds and the more exhausting the struggle becomes. Surrender is the choice to release the rope—not as an act of defeat, but as an act of wisdom. In letting go, you free yourself from the struggle and open yourself to new possibilities that could not emerge while entrenched in resistance.

Surrender and Acceptance

Surrender is an act of acceptance. It is the recognition that life is not something to be controlled but something to be experienced. When you accept life as it is instead of as you wish, you free yourself from the mental and emotional turmoil of resistance.

Acceptance does not mean agreeing with or condoning everything that happens. It means acknowledging the reality of the present moment without trying to change it. From this place of acceptance, you can respond to life with greater wisdom and intention, unclouded by the frustration and anger that come from resisting what is.

Surrender as Freedom

Surrender is also an act of liberation. When you let go of the need to control, you release yourself from the endless mental chatter of "what if" and "if only." You stop living in the past or projecting into the future and become fully present in the now.

In this space of surrender, you discover a profound sense of freedom. Your attachments no longer bind you to outcomes, your grievances about what has been, or your fears of what might be. You are free to experience life as it unfolds, moment by moment, with an open heart and a clear mind.

Surrender and Trust

Surrender also requires trust—a deep faith in the intelligence of life. The mind often resists surrender because it fears letting go means losing control. But the truth is that control is an illusion. Life is far too vast, intricate, and interconnected to be managed by the limited perspective of the human mind.

When you surrender, you are not relinquishing control to chaos. You are aligning yourself with the natural flow of existence—a flow that is far more intelligent and harmonious than anything the ego could orchestrate. Trusting in this flow allows you to move through life with greater ease and grace, knowing that even challenges and uncertainties have their place in the larger tapestry of your journey.

Surrender as Empowerment

Far from being a sign of weakness, surrender is a deeply empowering choice. It allows you to reclaim your energy from futile struggles and redirect it toward what truly matters. It frees you from the exhausting task of trying to control every detail of your life and opens you to the wisdom and possibilities that emerge when you let go.

When you surrender, you become your true strength—not the brittle strength of resistance, but the flexible, unshakable strength of presence and trust. You become like a tree that bends in the wind, resilient and rooted rather than rigid and easily broken. In surrendering, you find not loss but power—the power to live fully and authentically, unburdened by the illusion of control.

Reflection: Exploring the Strength of Surrender

What are you resisting in your life right now? Reflect on situations where you feel frustration, anger, or a need to control. What would happen if you chose to release your resistance?

How do you define strength? Consider whether your definition of strength includes surrender. How might embracing surrender expand your understanding of what it means to be strong?

Can you trust the flow of life? Reflect on moments when letting go led to unexpected clarity or solutions. How might trusting life's flow bring greater ease and freedom into your experience?

Why We Hold Onto Pain, Relationships, or Identities That No Longer Serve Us

Letting go is often described as a release, a freeing ourselves from burdens we no longer need to carry. Yet, if letting go is so liberating, why do we resist it? Why do we hold onto pain, relationships, and identities that no longer serve us? The answer lies in the mind's fear of loss, the ego's need for security, and our deep aversion to uncertainty.

We cling to what we know—even if it causes us suffering—because it feels familiar, safe, and predictable. On the other hand, letting go feels like stepping into the unknown, where the mind fears it will lose control and the ego fears it will lose itself.

The Familiarity of Pain

Pain, though unpleasant, can become a kind of comfort. It anchors us to the past, giving us a story to tell about who we are and why we are the way we are. Holding onto pain allows us to feel justified in our grievances and validated in our struggles. It becomes part of our identity: *I am the one who was hurt, the one who suffered.*

The mind resists letting go of pain because it fears that releasing it will cause us to lose a piece of ourselves. Who are we without our struggles? Without our wounds? The ego clings to pain as proof of its existence, reinforcing the illusion that we are defined by what has happened to us.

The Fear of Letting Go

The same fear applies to relationships and identities that no longer serve us. We hold onto relationships—even toxic ones—because they provide a sense of belonging or validation. Letting go of such relationships feels like stepping into loneliness or rejection, even when they cause more harm than good.

Similarly, we cling to outdated identities because they give us a sense of continuity and stability. We say, "This is who I am," even if that identity has become a cage. The ego fears change because it interprets it as a threat to its survival. It whispers: *If you let go, you will lose yourself.*

But here is the truth: letting go does not diminish you. It frees you. Pain, relationships, and identities are not who you are. They are experiences and roles you have carried, but they are not your essence. When you release them, you do not lose yourself; you uncover the self that exists beyond the stories, labels, and attachments.

The Illusion of Security

We often hold onto what no longer serves us because it gives us a false sense of security. Pain can feel like a shield, protecting us from further hurt by keeping us guarded. Toxic relationships can feel like anchors, grounding us even as they weigh us down. Identities can feel like a foundation, giving us a sense of self even when they confine us.

But this security is an illusion. Pain does not protect you—it keeps you trapped. Toxic relationships do not anchor you—they tether you to suffering. Identities do not define you—they limit your growth. True security comes not from holding on but from trusting in your ability to navigate life without these attachments.

The Freedom of Letting Go

You do not lose anything essential when you let go of what no longer serves you. Instead, you create space for something new—space for healing, growth, and the unfolding of your true self. Letting go is not an act of weakness; it is an act of strength and self-compassion. It is a declaration that you are no longer defined by your pain, bound by unhealthy relationships, or confined by outdated identities.

Letting go does not mean forgetting the past, abandoning relationships, or denying who you have been. It means recognizing that your essence is not bound by these things. It means stepping into the present moment and trusting that you are whole and complete, even without the things you once thought you needed to hold onto.

Living Without Attachments

To let go is to trust in the impermanence of life and the resilience of your true self. It is to see that you do not need pain, relationships, or identities to define you. Who you are is far greater than any experience, role, or attachment.

As you begin to let go, you may find that what you release does not leave a void but creates space—space for clarity, peace, and new possibilities. Letting go is not an end; it is a beginning. It is the gateway to freedom, growth, and the unfolding of your truest self.

...

We'd Love to Hear From You!

Thank you so much for reading this book-it means the world to me. If you found it helpful, inspiring, or just enjoyable, would you take a moment to leave a review? Your feedback not only helps others but also keeps me motivated to create more valuable content for you.

Here's how you can leave a review:

1. Scan the QR code on this page to go directly to the author's page.

2. Or, visit your Amazon Orders page, find this book, and click "Write a Product Review."

Your kind words make a big difference.
Thank you for your support!

Chapter Three

How Resistance to "What Is" Amplifies Suffering

"When you hold onto your history, you do it at the expense of your destiny."

— Bishop T.D. Jakes

Life unfolds moment by moment, indifferent to our preferences, plans, or expectations. Yet, instead of accepting what is, we often resist it. We resist the unpleasant circumstances, emotions we don't want to feel, and events we cannot control. This resistance may feel like an act of strength—a way of asserting control over life—but it is, in fact, the very source of much of our suffering.

Resistance does not change reality. It does not undo what has happened or prevent what is unfolding. Instead, it creates tension, amplifies discomfort, and keeps us locked in a battle with life itself. When we resist what is, we add a layer of suffering on top of the pain or challenge we are experiencing.

The Nature of Resistance

Resistance arises when we mentally or emotionally push back against reality. It is the thought: *This should not be happening.* It is the feeling of frustration, anger, or despair when life doesn't conform to our expectations.

Resistance often masquerades as control. The mind believes that we can change what is happening or avoid what we fear by resisting. But resistance is futile. It is like trying to hold back the ocean's waves. The waves will continue to crash regardless of your effort, and all you will achieve is exhaustion.

This does not mean that pain or difficulty should be passively endured. Pain is inevitable in life, but resistance is optional. Resistance—the mental pushback against pain—amplifies our suffering.

The Cycle of Resistance and Suffering

When we resist what is, we create a cycle of suffering that perpetuates itself.

For example:

> You feel sadness, but instead of allowing it, you resist it, thinking: *I shouldn't feel this way.* This resistance creates a secondary layer of frustration or self-judgment, which amplifies the sadness.

> You experience a challenging situation, but instead of accepting it, you resist it with thoughts like: *This isn't fair or shouldn't be happening.* This resistance turns the challenge into a source of ongoing mental and emotional turmoil.

> You make a mistake, and instead of learning from it, you resist it by replaying it in your mind,

wishing it could be undone. This resistance traps you in regret and prevents growth.

In each case, the original pain or challenge is compounded by resistance. The suffering is not in the event itself, but in the story the mind tells about it and the energy spent fighting it.

Why We Resist

Resistance is rooted in the ego's desire for control and the mind's aversion to discomfort. The ego believes it knows best—that life should unfold according to its preferences. When reality diverges from these expectations, the ego resists, insisting that life must conform to its desires.

The mind also resists because it fears discomfort. It does not want to feel pain, sadness, fear, or uncertainty. But in resisting these emotions, the mind inadvertently strengthens them. What we resist persists because resistance keeps our attention locked onto what we try to avoid.

The Power of Acceptance

The antidote to resistance is acceptance. Acceptance does not mean passivity or resignation; it means seeing reality clearly and allowing it to be as it is. It is the simple acknowledgment: *This is what is happening right now.*

Acceptance does not condone or approve of everything. It does not mean you must agree with or like what is happening. It simply means you stop fighting reality and instead allow yourself to meet it as it is. In doing so, you free yourself from the additional suffering resistance creates.

Acceptance as Liberation

When you accept what is, you create a space of clarity and

peace. You are no longer trapped in the mental struggle of resistance, and you can respond to life from a place of wisdom rather than reactivity.

For example:

> When you accept your emotions, you allow them to move through you rather than becoming stuck. Sadness, anger, or fear lose their grip when faced with openness rather than resistance.

> When you accept a challenging situation, you stop wasting energy wishing it were different. Instead, you can focus on what you can do in the present moment to navigate it.

> When you accept mistakes or setbacks, you free yourself from regret and open the door to growth and learning.

Resistance Is Futile–But Acceptance Is Freedom

Life will continue to unfold as it will, regardless of whether we resist or accept it. Resistance changes nothing about the external world; it only creates internal conflict. Acceptance, on the other hand, transforms our relationship with life. It allows us to engage with reality as it is rather than as we wish it to be.

Ask yourself:

> *What would my life look like if I stopped resisting?*

> *What energy would be freed if I accepted what is?*

To accept is not to give up; it is to step into the flow of life with strength and clarity. It is to let go of the futile struggle against reality and to discover the peace and freedom that have always been available in the present moment

Resistance: Swimming Upstream Versus Flowing with the Current

Imagine yourself in a river. The current moves steadily, carrying everything in its flow—branches, leaves, and even the occasional obstacle. This river is life itself, always in motion, always moving forward. When you resist life, it's as though you are swimming upstream against the current. Every stroke demands immense effort, yet the river remains indifferent to your struggle. The current keeps flowing, and no matter how hard you swim, you find yourself exhausted, frustrated, and no closer to your destination.

Now, imagine instead allowing yourself to float with the current. The river carries you effortlessly, and though you may encounter rocks or eddies along the way, you move with the natural flow rather than against it. The obstacles do not disappear, but they no longer feel like insurmountable barriers. You navigate them easily because you are not wasting all your energy fighting the current.

This is the essence of resistance versus surrender. Resistance is the act of swimming upstream, fueled by the belief that we can bend life to our will. Surrender is the choice to flow with life, trusting its intelligence to carry us where we need to go.

The Futility of Swimming Upstream

Swimming upstream may feel like strength, but it is an exercise in futility. Life is vast, dynamic, and beyond the control of any single individual. To resist its flow is to pit yourself against forces far greater than yourself. It is to expend energy on a battle you cannot win.

When you resist, you become fixated on controlling outcomes, altering circumstances, or avoiding discomfort. But this fixation blinds you to the wisdom of the current, the natural unfolding of life. Like a swimmer who fights the river, you exhaust yourself while the current carries on, unchanged and unbothered by your struggle.

Resistance not only drains your energy but also limits your perspective. In your effort to swim upstream, your focus narrows to the fight itself. You lose sight of the broader landscape, the opportunities and beauty that exist all around you. The river is not your enemy; it is your path. To resist it is to miss the journey altogether.

The Power of Flowing with the Current

Flowing with the current does not mean passively drifting or surrendering to every wave and obstacle without agency. It means aligning yourself with the natural rhythm of life. It means recognizing that while you cannot control the river's flow, you can choose how you move within it.

To flow with the current is to trust life. It is to let go of the belief that you must have all the answers or dictate every turn. Trust does not eliminate challenges but transforms your relationship with them. When you flow with the current, obstacles become navigable rather than overwhelming. You see them for what they are—temporary events, not insurmountable barriers.

The river knows its course. It winds through valleys, carves paths through mountains, and eventually finds its way to the ocean. Trusting the river does not mean you know exactly where it will take you, but you are willing to let it carry you, trusting that its course has purpose and direction.

Resistance as Fear of Letting Go

Resistance often arises from fear—the fear of losing control, being swept away by the unknown, and facing the discomfort that comes with uncertainty. The mind equates resistance with safety, as though clinging to the riverbank will prevent you from being carried into uncharted waters.

But clinging to the riverbank only delays the inevitable. Life will continue to flow, and the longer you hold on, the more you feel the tension of being pulled in two directions—toward the future and your refusal to move forward.

Letting go requires trust, not only in the river but in your ability to navigate its waters. It is an acknowledgment that while you cannot control the current, you can meet whatever arises with presence and grace. Letting go is not weakness but the ultimate strength—the strength to release fear and embrace the unknown.

A Profound Metaphor: The River as Life's Wisdom

The river symbolizes life's flow and reflects its wisdom. The current does not resist obstacles; it moves around, over, and sometimes through them. It finds the path of least resistance and adapts to the terrain without losing its momentum.

In this way, the river teaches us how to live. When you encounter a challenge, ask yourself: *Am I fighting this obstacle, or am I allowing myself to flow around it?* Resistance hardens you, but flow softens you, allowing you to adapt and grow.

The river also teaches us about impermanence. No part of the river is ever the same; it is always changing, always moving. To cling to one moment in the river's flow is to deny its nature. Similarly, clinging to moments, people, or outcomes in life is to resist its inherent impermanence. Letting go allows you to embrace the flow and experience life fully without being weighed down by what has already passed.

Living in Alignment with the Current

To live in alignment with the current is to live in harmony with life itself. It means recognizing that resistance is not a sign of strength but of fear. Strength lies in your ability to release resistance and move with life, trusting in its intelligence and your resilience.

Ask yourself:

Where am I swimming upstream in my life?

What would it feel like to release the struggle and let the current carry me?

When you stop fighting the river, you do not lose control; you gain freedom. You open yourself to the flow of life, discovering that it is not a force to be resisted but a journey to be embraced.

Presence as the Antidote to Resistance

Resistance thrives on the mind's tendency to dwell in the past or project into the future. It feeds on thoughts like *This shouldn't have happened* or *What if this gets worse?* By anchoring itself in these mental projections, resistance keeps you locked in a state of conflict with reality.

Presence, however, dissolves resistance. When you are fully present in the moment, there is no space for past regrets or future fears. The mind quiets, and the energy once consumed by resistance is redirected into awareness. Presence brings you into direct contact with life as it is, without the filters of judgment, expectation, or denial. In this state, resistance loses its power, and you find clarity, peace, and the ability to respond to life with ease.

What Is Presence?

Presence is not something you create or achieve; it is your natural state when you are not consumed by thought. It is the simple act of being here, fully aware of this moment, without distraction or resistance. Presence is the space where life unfolds—the only place where reality exists. The past is gone, the future is not yet here, and the present moment is all there is.

When you are present, you do not think about what has happened or what might happen. You simply experience what is. You notice the sensations in your body, the sounds around you, and the rhythm of your breath. This awareness grounds you and pulls you out of the mental loops that fuel resistance.

How Presence Dissolves Resistance

Resistance requires thought to exist. It is built on mental narratives—stories about how things should be, could have been, or might become. Presence, on the other hand, requires no thought. It is the direct experience of life, free from interpretation or judgment.

When you bring your attention fully to the present moment, resistance can no longer take hold. Without the stories of the mind, there is nothing to resist. You are simply here, experiencing life as it is. In this state, even pain loses its sting because it is no longer amplified by mental resistance. Pain becomes a sensation, not a story.

The Stillness Within Presence

Presence is often described as stillness—not the absence of

movement, but the absence of internal conflict. In presence, you are no longer pushing against reality or trying to escape it. You are simply observing, allowing, and accepting. This stillness does not mean passivity; it is an alert, dynamic state in which you fully engage with life without resistance.

Imagine standing in the middle of a storm. Resistance is like trying to fight the wind, pushing against its force, and exhausting yourself. Presence is like standing still, feeling the wind move around you, observing its power without trying to control it. The storm may continue, but you are no longer caught in its turmoil.

Presence as Strength

Being present is not always easy, especially when faced with discomfort or challenge. The mind will try to pull you into resistance, convincing you that the only way to solve a problem is to fight against it. But presence is the true source of strength. It allows you to face whatever arises without being overwhelmed by it. In presence, you find the clarity and calm to respond, rather than react.

For example:

> When faced with pain, presence allows you to experience it directly without adding the mental layers of resistance that turn pain into suffering.

> When dealing with a challenging situation, presence keeps you grounded, enabling you to see the situation clearly and act with wisdom rather than from a place of fear or frustration.

> When navigating uncertainty, presence frees you from the anxiety of "what if" by anchoring you in

the reality of "what is."

Presence and the Flow of Life

Life itself is always present. The river of life does not flow backward into the past or forward into the future; it exists only in this moment. To resist the present is to resist life itself. But when you align yourself with presence, you move with the flow of life. You stop swimming upstream against the current of reality and instead allow yourself to be carried by it.

This alignment does not mean passively accepting everything that happens. Presence gives you the clarity to discern when action is needed and the strength to take that action without resistance. It is a state of flow in which you are fully engaged with life yet unburdened by the mental noise that clouds your perception.

Presence and Peace

Peace is not something you achieve by changing your circumstances; it is something you uncover by being present. In the absence of resistance, peace arises naturally. It depends not on external conditions but on your relationship with this moment. You are no longer caught in the past or future when you are present. You are free from the stories that create suffering, and you find yourself resting in the stillness of now.

Living in Presence

To live in presence is to live in freedom. It means to meet life as it is, moment by moment, without resistance or judgment. Presence does not deny life's challenges; it allows you to face them with strength and clarity, unburdened by resistance's mental and emotional weight.

Ask yourself: *What would it feel like to simply be here, in this moment, without resistance?* Let the mind quiet, the body relax, and life unfold. In this space of presence, you discover that resistance is unnecessary and peace has always been available, waiting for you to notice it.

Chapter Four

Awareness is the Key

"Awareness is the greatest agent for change."

— Eckhart Tolle

Observing Your Thoughts and Emotions Without Judgment

The mind is an endless stream of thoughts, a constant chatter that narrates, analyzes, and evaluates every moment of your experience. Emotions rise and fall like waves, often influenced by the stories your mind creates. For most people, these thoughts and emotions are not simply passing experiences; they are mistaken for truth, reality, and self. But here is the liberating truth: you are not your thoughts, nor are you your emotions. You are the awareness in which they arise and subside.

To step into this awareness, you must first learn to observe your thoughts and emotions without judgment. This is not about suppressing or changing them but about creating space between you and the mental and emotional activity that often consumes you. In this space, you discover the freedom to see your inner world as it is—not as a reflection of who you are, but as a transient part of your human experience.

The Power of Observation

Observation is a simple but profound practice. When you observe your thoughts and emotions, you create a shift in perspective. Instead of being caught up in them, you become the witness. This witnessing is not passive; it is an act of presence, a way of stepping out of the mind's habitual identification with its content.

When anger arises, the mind often latches onto it, feeding it with thoughts like: *This is unfair. I have a right to feel this way.* Without realizing it, you become the anger. It colors your perception, your actions, and your sense of self. But when you observe anger as it arises—*Ah, anger is here; I feel its heat, its tightness in my chest*—you create a space between the emotion and your identity. You are no longer the anger; you are the awareness observing it.

Why Judgment Keeps You Stuck

The mind loves to judge. It labels thoughts as good or bad, emotions as positive or negative, and experiences as right or wrong. This judgment reinforces the ego's need to control and categorize, creating resistance and suffering.

When you judge a thought or emotion, you add another layer to it.

For example:

A thought arises: *I made a mistake.*

Judgment follows: *I'm so careless; I'll never get it right.*

This judgment amplifies the original thought, trapping you in a cycle of self-criticism and resistance.

Judgment turns fleeting thoughts and emotions into fixed identities. But when you observe without judgment, you break this cycle. You allow the thought or emotion to simply be without attaching meaning or identity. In this way, observation becomes an act of liberation.

The Nature of Thoughts and Emotions

Thoughts and emotions are not who you are. They are temporary phenomena that arise in the field of your awareness. Like clouds passing through the sky, they come and go, constantly changing shape and intensity. Some are fleeting, like a wisp of vapor; others linger, like storm clouds. But none of them stay forever.

When you observe your inner world, you begin to see this transience. You realize that no thought or emotion defines you because they are not permanent. They are simply experiences moving through the vast space of your awareness. You are not the clouds; you are the sky.

How to Observe Without Judgment

Observing your thoughts and emotions without judgment is a practice of presence and curiosity. It requires attention, openness, and the willingness to let go of your habitual identification with the mind.

> **Pause and Notice.** When a thought or emotion arises, pause for a moment. Instead of reacting or suppressing it, bring your attention to it. Notice its qualities—its texture, intensity, and movement.

> **Name It Without Judgment.** Give the thought or

emotion a simple label: This is fear, or This is worry. Naming it helps you create distance, allowing you to observe without getting entangled.

Feel It in Your Body. Thoughts often trigger emotions, and emotions manifest in the body. Where do you feel it? Is there tightness, warmth, or pressure? Observe the sensation without trying to change it.

Let It Be. Resist the urge to push the thought or emotion away or to cling to it. Let it arise, exist, and fade in its own time. Trust that it will pass, as all thoughts and emotions do.

Return to Presence. Once you have observed the thought or emotion, return your attention to the present moment. Focus on your breath, the sounds around you, or the sensations in your body. This anchors you in the now.

The Freedom of Observation

When you observe your thoughts and emotions without judgment, you step into your true nature: awareness. This awareness is not reactive; it is still, spacious, and free. It holds everything without being affected by anything. In this space of observation, you discover that you are not the turbulence of the mind; you are the calm presence in which it arises.

As you practice observation, you may notice a profound shift. Thoughts and emotions that once felt overwhelming lose their grip. They no longer dominate your experience or define your identity. You begin to move through life with greater ease and clarity, unburdened by the weight of your inner chatter.

Ask yourself: *What would it feel like to simply observe my thoughts and emotions without needing to change or judge them?* In this practice, you may find a freedom that has always been within you, waiting to be noticed.

Awareness: The Bridge Between Suffering and Liberation

For most people, suffering feels inevitable, as though it were an inescapable part of life. It arises from the stories the mind tells, the emotions it amplifies, and the resistance it creates. But suffering is not inherent to life. It is a product of identification—identifying with the thoughts, emotions, and narratives that pass through your mind. To be free of suffering, you must step out of identification and into awareness.

Awareness is the bridge. It spans the chasm between suffering and liberation, between the entanglement of the mind and the stillness of being. Awareness is not something you acquire or achieve; it is your natural state, obscured only by the noise of the mind. When you reconnect with awareness, you begin to see suffering for what it is—a mental construct, not a fundamental truth. Through this recognition, you find liberation.

What Is Awareness?

Awareness is the silent observer within you. It is the presence that notices your thoughts, emotions, and experiences without becoming entangled in them. It is not thought, nor is it a product of the mind. Awareness exists beyond the mind, untouched by the stories and judgments the mind creates.

Imagine standing on a hill, watching the traffic below. Cars come and go, some moving quickly, others slowly. You do not chase after the cars or try to stop them; you simply observe. Awareness is like this—a vantage point from which you can watch the thoughts and emotions that pass through you without being carried away by them. From this perspective, you begin to see that you are not the traffic but the one observing it.

How Awareness Dissolves Suffering

Suffering cannot survive in the light of awareness. To suffer, you must believe the thoughts and emotions that arise within you. You must identify with them, giving them power and permanence. Awareness breaks this identification. It allows you to see thoughts and emotions as transient phenomena, not as truths or as reflections of who you are.

For example:

> When you feel anxiety, the mind might say: *This is unbearable. Something terrible is going to happen.* If you are unaware, you believe this thought and become consumed by the anxiety. But in awareness, you step back and notice: *Ah, there is anxiety.* There is a thought about the future. You see the thought and the emotion for what they are—passing events in the field of your awareness. The anxiety may still be present, but it no longer controls   you.

> When you feel anger, awareness allows you to observe its rise and fall. Instead of acting on or suppressing the anger, you simply notice: *There is anger here.* This observation creates space, and the anger begins to lose intensity in that space. Without identification, it fades naturally.

In this way, awareness dissolves suffering by removing the fuel that sustains it: identification.

Awareness as Liberation

Liberation is not something you achieve in the future; it is something you realize in the present. It is not an escape from life's challenges but a new way of relating to them. When you live in awareness, you are no longer at the mercy of the mind's stories. You are free to experience life as it is without the layers of resistance, judgment, and attachment that create suffering.

Awareness liberates you from the past and future, anchoring you in the now. It frees you from the need to control, to cling, or to resist. In awareness, you discover that life is not a problem to be solved but a reality to be experienced fully and freely.

The Bridge Between the Mind and Being

The mind is a powerful tool, but it is not who you are. It operates in the realm of thought, judgment, and duality, dividing life into good and bad, right and wrong, past and future. Awareness, on the other hand, operates in the realm of being. It is the stillness beneath the activity of the mind, the space in which all thoughts and experiences arise.

Awareness acts as a bridge between the mind and being. When you are lost in the mind, you live in a state of suffering, constantly judging, resisting, or clinging to life. But when you step into awareness, you cross the bridge into being, where suffering dissolves, and you experience life as it is—whole, complete, and free.

The Simplicity of Awareness

Awareness does not require effort. It is not something you must figure out or force into existence. It is already here, always present, waiting for you to notice. The only reason awareness feels elusive is that the mind's chatter drowns it out. But the moment you bring your attention to the present moment, awareness reveals itself.

Try this now: Pause for a moment and simply notice your breath. Feel the air moving in and out of your body. Notice the sensations in your hands or the sounds around you. In this simple act of noticing, you step into awareness. You are no longer lost in thought; you are present. This is the bridge.

Life in Awareness

When you live in awareness, you experience a profound shift. Suffering no longer feels inevitable. Challenges still arise, but they do not consume you. Thoughts and emotions still come, but they do not define you. You begin to see life as it truly is—impermanent, ever-changing, yet full of beauty and possibility.

The bridge of awareness is always available to you. No matter how entangled you feel in the mind's stories, you can step into awareness in any moment. Simply pause, notice, and observe. This is the doorway to liberation, the path to freedom. All it requires is your willingness to see.

Practical Self-Reflection Prompts to Identify Your Burdens

To step onto the path of awareness and liberation, you must first recognize what weighs you down. Burdens take many forms—thoughts, emotions, beliefs, attachments, or unresolved experiences. These burdens often operate in the background, shaping your perceptions and reactions without conscious awareness.

The following prompts are designed to help you bring these burdens to light so you can begin releasing them.

Recognizing Emotional Burdens

» What emotions frequently resurface in my life? Are there patterns of anger, sadness, fear, or resentment I have carried for a long time?

» When I think about the past, are there specific memories or experiences that still feel unresolved or painful?

» Do I find myself avoiding certain feelings or situations because they are uncomfortable? What might I be resisting?

Identifying Mental Patterns

» What repetitive thoughts occupy my mind? Are there stories I tell myself about who I am or how life should be?

» Do I often think in terms of "should have," "could have," or "if only"? How do these thoughts affect my experience of the present moment?

» Am I holding onto judgments about myself or others? What beliefs about these judgments keep them alive?

Examining Relationships

» Are there relationships in my life that feel draining, one-sided, or toxic? What am I holding onto in these relationships, and why?

» Do I fear letting go of certain connections because of what it might mean for my identity or sense of belonging?

» Am I clinging to past versions of relationships—how they once were or how I wish they could be—rather than accepting them as they are?

Exploring Attachments to Identity

» What roles, labels, or identities do I cling to most strongly? (e.g., my job, my family role, my achievements, my failures.)

» Do I feel defined by certain aspects of my past—my struggles, successes, or mistakes? How do these definitions limit me?

» What parts of my identity feel restrictive, as though they are cages rather than sources of freedom?

Understanding Resistance

» What am I currently resisting in my life? Are there situations, emotions, or truths I am unwilling to face?

» What fears underlie my resistance? Am I afraid of change, uncertainty, or losing control?

» What would it feel like to let go of this resistance? What might I gain in doing so?

Uncovering Beliefs About Control

» Do I believe I need to control every aspect of my life to feel safe or successful? Where does this belief come from?

» Are there situations or outcomes I am trying to force or manipulate? How is this effort affecting me emotionally and physically?

» What would it look like to trust the natural flow of life instead of clinging to control?

Reflecting on Physical Tension

» Where in my body do I often feel tension, tightness, or discomfort? Could this be a physical manifestation of emotional or mental burdens?

» What happens when I bring my attention to these areas of tension? Does the sensation change when I simply observe it without judgment?

» How might releasing physical tension help me connect with the deeper emotional or mental burdens I am carrying?

Discovering What No Longer Serves You

» What in my life feels heavy, stagnant, or outdated? Are there habits, routines, or commitments that no longer align with who I am becoming?

» Are there goals or aspirations I am holding onto out of obligation or fear rather than genuine desire?

» What would my life feel like if I let go of the things that no longer serve me?

Connecting to the Present Moment

» How much of my mental energy is spent dwelling on the past or worrying about the future?

» What parts of my day do I fully experience with my complete attention? How often am I distracted by thoughts of "what was" or "what might be"?

» What would it feel like to focus entirely on this moment?

Clarifying Your Desire for Freedom

» What does freedom mean to me? How do I envision freedom in my thoughts, emotions, relationships, and daily life?

» What is currently standing between me and that freedom? Are these barriers external, internal, or both?

» Am I willing to release what burdens me in order to experience freedom? If not, what fears or beliefs are holding me back?

Integrating Reflection Into Awareness

Use these prompts as an ongoing practice. Set aside time each day or week to explore one or more questions. Write down your answers, and allow yourself to observe them without judgment.

Awareness begins with noticing—what arises, how it feels, and how it shapes your experience. In this act of noticing, you take the first step toward liberation.

Chapter Five

The Ego's Role: Thriving on Attachment and Conflict

"What you resist not only persists but will grow in size."

— Carl Jung

The ego is not an entity but a mental construct—a collection of thoughts, beliefs, and identities that create the illusion of a separate self. It thrives on attachment and conflict because these serve to reinforce its sense of existence. The ego cannot survive in stillness or presence. It needs constant activity: stories to tell, dramas to engage in, and attachments to protect. In its pursuit of control and self-preservation, the ego creates conflict both internally and externally, trapping us in a cycle of resistance and suffering.

Understanding the ego's role in attachment and conflict is essential for liberation. When you begin to see how the ego operates, you create distance between yourself and its narratives. This distance is awareness—the space in which freedom becomes possible.

The Ego and Attachment

The ego thrives on attachment because attachment gives it something to cling to, something to define itself by. It attaches to roles, possessions, relationships, achievements, and even pain. Each attachment becomes a thread in the tapestry of the ego's identity, weaving a story of *who I am and what I need to be complete*.

For example:

> The ego says: *I am my success.* When success is achieved, the ego swells with pride; when it is lost, the ego feels threatened and diminished.

> The ego says: *I am my relationships.* It clings to people, demanding validation and fearing abandonment. Relationships become sources of control and dependency rather than mutual connection.

> The ego says: *I am my pain.* It identifies with wounds and grievances, using them to define itself as a victim. In this way, even suffering becomes an attachment.

The problem with attachment is not the things themselves—success, relationships, or even pain—but the ego's need to derive identity and worth from them. Attachment creates fear: fear of loss, fear of failure, fear of change. The ego resists letting go because to lose an attachment feels like losing a piece of itself.

The Ego and Conflict

The ego also thrives on conflict. Conflict strengthens the illusion of separateness, reinforcing the idea that there is *me* and *the other, right* and *wrong, mine* and *theirs.* The ego craves this division because it defines itself in opposition to others. Without conflict, the ego begins to dissolve.

Consider how the ego creates conflict:

Inwardly, it generates self-criticism and doubt. It tells you: *You're not good enough, or You need to be better.* This inner conflict keeps you striving, always feeling incomplete.

Outwardly, it projects judgment and blame. It says: *They are wrong, or They should change.* This external conflict fuels resentment, anger, and separation.

The ego's attachment to conflict lies in a deeper mechanism: its use of fear and identity to anchor you in the past. By engaging in conflict, the ego feels powerful and significant. The ego knows that if you remain tethered to past stories and fears, it can maintain its hold on your sense of self. Understanding this is key to recognizing how the ego perpetuates suffering.

The Ego's Fear of Dissolution

The ego fears awareness because awareness dissolves its hold. When you step into awareness, you begin to see the ego's patterns of attachment and conflict for what they are—mental constructs, not reflections of reality. This recognition threatens the ego's existence.

To protect itself, the ego creates distractions. It keeps you focused on the past or future, away from the present moment where awareness resides. It amplifies thoughts and emotions, keeping you entangled in its narratives. It resists stillness, fearing the silence in which its illusions unravel.

The ego's fear of dissolution is why letting go feels so difficult. To release attachment or conflict requires stepping beyond the ego's realm into the unknown. The ego interprets this as a threat, convincing you that without it, you will lose yourself. But the truth is, you do not lose yourself when the ego dissolves; you discover the deeper self that has always been present beneath it.

How the Ego Perpetuates Suffering

The ego's attachments and conflicts are the root of much of our suffering. Here's how:

> **Attachment to Outcomes:** The ego resists uncertainty, clinging to specific outcomes to feel secure. When life does not go as planned, the ego creates frustration and disappointment.

> **Attachment to Identity:** The ego defines itself by roles, achievements, and stories. When these identities are challenged or lost, the ego feels threatened, creating fear and grief.

> **Conflict with Reality:** The ego resists what is, insisting that life conforms to its expectations. This resistance amplifies pain and creates inner turmoil.

> **Conflict with Others:** The ego seeks to assert itself by judging, blaming, or controlling others. This external conflict creates division and perpetuates cycles of suffering.

The ego perpetuates suffering because it cannot accept the impermanence and unpredictability of life. It clings, resists, and fights, creating tension and disconnection. In contrast, awareness brings clarity and freedom. It reveals that the suffering created by the ego is unnecessary—a product of identification, not reality.

Awareness as the Antidote to the Ego

The ego thrives in unconsciousness. It needs you to remain unaware, entangled in its narratives, for it to survive. Awareness is the antidote. When you become aware of the ego's patterns, you step out of identification with them. You begin to see: *This is not who I am. This is just a thought, a belief, an emotion passing through me.*

Awareness allows you to observe the ego's attachments and conflicts without being drawn into them. You see the ego trying to hold on, trying to create drama, and you recognize it for what it is—a mental construct, not your true self.

With awareness, you begin to release the ego's grip. Attachments lose their intensity because you no longer see them as essential to your identity. Conflict dissolves because you no longer need to prove or defend yourself. In the space of awareness, the ego's illusions fade, and you discover the freedom and peace that were always present beneath them.

Moving Beyond the Ego

To move beyond the ego is not to destroy it but to stop identifying with it. The ego will still arise, as it is part of the human experience. But with awareness, it no longer controls you. You can see its patterns, smile at its attempts to assert itself, and let it go.

Ask yourself:

What attachments am I clinging to?

What conflicts am I engaged in?

How does the ego fuel these patterns in my life?

As you bring awareness to these questions, you take the first step toward liberation. The ego thrives on attachment and conflict, but it cannot survive in the light of awareness. And in that light, you find the bridge to peace, freedom, and your true self.

How the Ego Uses Fear and Identity to Keep Us Stuck in the Past

The ego's survival depends on its ability to tether you to an identity rooted in time. It thrives on your attachment to the past—your stories, wounds, achievements, and failures—because the past gives the ego its sense of "self." Without these stories, the ego has nothing to sustain itself. And so, it weaves a web of fear and identity, keeping you stuck in a narrative that prevents you from stepping into the freedom of the present moment.

Fear and identity are the ego's primary tools. Together, they create an illusion of permanence and control, convincing you that letting go of the past means losing yourself. The truth, however, is that your true self is not found in the past. It exists only in the now, beyond the ego's constructs.

The Ego's Use of Fear

The ego uses fear as a defense mechanism, ensuring that you remain bound to its narrative. Fear serves two primary functions for the ego:

> **Fear of Letting Go:** The ego convinces you that letting go of the past is dangerous. It whispers: *If you release this pain, who will you be? If you let go of this identity, you will have nothing left.* The ego equates letting go with annihilation, creating a deep resistance to change.

For example, if your identity is tied to a past wound—*I was wronged, and this defines who I am*—the ego fears that releasing the wound will leave you without a story, without a purpose. It clings to the pain, not because it serves you but because it sustains the ego's sense of self.

Fear of Repetition: The ego uses past experiences as a template for the future, constantly projecting fear onto what might happen. It says: *You failed before; you will fail again. You were hurt before; you will be hurt again.* By keeping you focused on the past, the ego ensures that you remain in a state of hyper-vigilance, trying to avoid the perceived dangers of the future. This fear traps you in a cycle of anxiety and avoidance, preventing you from experiencing the freedom of the present.

The Ego's Attachment to Identity

The ego thrives on identity because identity provides structure and continuity. It needs a story to tell about who you are—one that ties together your past experiences, roles, and labels into a cohesive narrative. This identity becomes the ego's foundation, a false sense of self that it defends at all costs.

The Identity of the Wounded Self: Many people carry an identity tied to their pain. The ego says: *I am my suffering. I am the person who was betrayed, abandoned, or mistreated.* While this identity may feel justified, it also becomes a prison. The ego uses it to keep you stuck in the past, replaying the same stories and emotions and reinforcing the idea that you are defined by what happened to you.

The Identity of the Achiever: The ego also clings to positive identities—*I am my success. I am my accomplishments.* While this identity may seem empowering, it is equally limiting. It ties your worth to external outcomes, creating fear of failure and loss. The ego resists change because it sees any threat to this identity as a threat to your existence.

The Identity of Roles: The ego attaches itself to roles—parent, professional, victim, healer—defining you by what you do rather than who you are. These roles may feel secure, but they also create rigidity. When circumstances shift or roles change, the ego feels destabilized, clinging to the past version of yourself to avoid facing the uncertainty of the present.

How Fear and Identity Keep You Stuck in the Past

The combination of fear and identity creates a feedback loop that binds you to the past:

The ego uses fear to keep you from questioning or releasing the stories that define you. It says: *This pain, this role, this achievement—it's who you are. Without it, you will be nothing.*

It reinforces these stories by tying them to your identity. It says: *You are your pain, your mistakes, your successes. These are what make you valuable, meaningful, or safe.*

The fear of losing this identity keeps you clinging to the past, replaying old narratives, and resisting the natural flow of life.

This cycle prevents you from seeing the present moment clearly. Instead of experiencing life as it is, you experience it through the lens of the past, projecting old fears and attachments onto new situations.

The Illusion of the Ego's Fear and Identity

The ego's use of fear and identity is based on an illusion. It convinces you that your past defines you, that you are your thoughts, emotions, and experiences. But when you step into awareness, you begin to see that these are not who you are—they are simply stories created by the mind.

Fear is not a reflection of reality; it is a reaction to a mental projection. Identity is not a reflection of your true self; it is a construct of the ego. The more you identify with these illusions, the more you remain stuck in the past. But the moment you recognize them for what they are, the grip of the ego begins to loosen.

Breaking Free: Awareness and Presence

To free yourself from the ego's hold, you must step into awareness. Awareness allows you to observe the ego's patterns without being controlled by them. When fear arises, awareness lets you see it as a passing emotion, not a truth. When the ego clings to identity, awareness allows you to question its validity and see beyond it.

Presence dissolves the ego's attachment to the past. In the present moment, the stories of the past lose their power. You are no longer defined by what happened to you or by the roles you have played. Instead, you experience the freedom of being—your true self, unburdened by the mind's constructs.

A Reflection

Ask yourself:

What stories about my past is the ego clinging to? How do these stories shape my identity?

What fears arise when I consider letting go of these stories? Are these fears grounded in reality, or are they projections of the ego?

What would it feel like to release these stories and step into the present moment, free of the ego's grip?

Once you see how the ego uses fear and identity to bind you to the past, you begin to realize that these patterns are not who you are. This recognition is the first step toward freedom. By observing the ego's patterns without judgment, you create the space to break free from its grip.

Freedom Begins When We Recognize the Ego's Patterns

The ego thrives in the shadows of unawareness. Its survival depends on your unconscious identification with its patterns— its stories, attachments, fears, and judgments. As long as you remain unaware of the ego's workings, you are at its mercy, living out the narratives it creates without question. But the moment you begin to recognize the ego for what it is, a shift occurs. Awareness begins to dawn, and with it comes freedom.

This freedom is not something the ego can give you, for the ego is the very source of the bondage. Freedom arises when you step into awareness when you become the observer of the ego rather than its puppet. To recognize the ego's patterns is to loosen its grip on your life, to see that the stories it tells are not reality, and to discover the spaciousness of being that exists beyond its constructs.

The Ego Thrives on Unconsciousness

The ego operates in the background, subtly influencing your thoughts, emotions, and actions. It thrives on your identification with its patterns:

> When the ego creates a story of victimhood, you believe: *This is who I am.*

> When the ego stirs up fear, you react like the threat is real.

> When the ego judges others, you accept its judgments without question, fueling division and conflict.

In unconsciousness, these patterns feel natural, even necessary. You do not see them as the ego; you see them as yourself. This identification keeps you trapped in cycles of resistance, suffering, and limitation because the ego's primary goal is not freedom but self-preservation.

Recognition Dissolves the Ego

The moment you recognize the ego's patterns, they begin to lose their power. Recognition is a light that shines on the shadows of the mind, exposing the ego's strategies and revealing them as mental constructs rather than truths.

For instance:

> When the ego says: *You need this person's approval to feel worthy*, awareness allows you to pause and see the thought for what it is: a conditioned belief, not a reflection of reality.

When the ego creates anxiety about the future, awareness lets you step back and observe: *Ah, this is fear arising. It is not the future; it is a thought in this moment.*

This recognition creates space. In that space, you are no longer identified with the ego's patterns. You become the observer, the awareness that sees the patterns without being controlled by them. In this state of presence, the ego begins to dissolve because it can no longer operate in the light of awareness.

The Ego's Patterns Are Predictable

The ego may seem complex, but its patterns are predictable. It uses the same strategies over and over:

Attachment: The ego clings to roles, possessions, and relationships, believing they define its worth.

Judgment: The ego divides life into good and bad, right and wrong, creating conflict and resistance.

Fear: The ego projects imagined threats onto the future, keeping you in a state of anxiety.

Comparison: The ego constantly measures itself against others, seeking superiority or lamenting inferiority.

Blame: The ego externalizes responsibility, pointing to others as the cause of its discomfort.

These patterns are not unique to you; they are universal to the human condition. By recognizing them, you begin to see that they are not personal. They are not "yours"; they are simply the ego's habitual ways of operating. This depersonalization is a key step toward freedom because it allows you to observe the ego without judgment or attachment.

Freedom Lies in the Space of Awareness

When you recognize the ego's patterns, you create a gap—a space between the thought or emotion and your sense of self. In that space, freedom arises. You are no longer bound by the ego's narratives because you see them for what they are: temporary phenomena passing through the field of awareness.

For example:

> A thought arises: *I am not good enough.* In un-consciousness, you believe this thought and feel its weight. In awareness, you recognize it as a passing thought, not a statement of truth.

> An emotion arises: Anger. In unconsciousness, you act on the *anger,* lashing out or suppressing it. In awareness, you observe the emotion without reacting, allowing it to rise and fall naturally.

In this space of awareness, you realize that the ego's patterns do not define you. They are like waves on the surface of the ocean—dynamic but impermanent. Beneath them lies the stillness of your true being, untouched by the turbulence of the mind.

The Ego's Resistance to Awareness

The ego resists recognition because it fears its own dissolution. It will distract you, amplify emotions, or create new narratives to pull you back into identification. It might say: *This is too difficult. You will never be free. Awareness won't solve your problems.*

This resistance is simply another pattern to observe. When you notice the ego resisting awareness, you are already stepping into awareness. Even the ego's resistance cannot stop the process of recognition once it begins.

Living in Awareness

Recognizing the ego's patterns is not a one-time event; it is an ongoing practice. Each moment of awareness deepens your freedom. Over time, the ego's patterns lose their intensity. They still arise, but they no longer dominate your experience. You see them, acknowledge them, and let them go.

In this way, awareness becomes your natural state. You live not as the ego but as the awareness in which the ego arises. This is freedom—not freedom from life's challenges, but freedom from the suffering created by the mind's identification with the ego.

A Reflection

Ask yourself:

What patterns of thought or behavior do I notice recurring in my life? How do these patterns keep me stuck?

When a thought or emotion arises, can I pause and observe it without judgment? What happens when I do?

What would it feel like to live from awareness rather than identification with the ego?

Awareness shines a light on the ego's patterns, allowing you to see the stories and attachments that have kept you stuck. But recognition alone is not enough; you must also confront the cost of holding on. What price are you paying to keep resentment, guilt, or fear alive?

Chapter Six

The Cost of Holding On

"When you realize nothing is lacking, the whole world belongs to you."

— Lao Tzu

To hold onto resentment, guilt, or fear is to burden yourself with unnecessary weight. Though natural when they arise, these emotions become destructive when clung to, like carrying heavy stones in your pockets as you attempt to swim. The mind, led by the ego, insists on keeping them alive, weaving narratives around them to justify their presence. But holding on comes at a cost that is often invisible until you step back and see the toll it has taken on your peace, freedom, and connection to life.

When we hold on, we tie ourselves to the past or project imagined fears onto the future, robbing the present moment of its vitality. Resentment poisons our relationships, guilt chains us to what cannot be undone, and fear paralyzes us from moving forward. To cling to these emotions is to resist life's natural flow, and in that resistance lies suffering.

The Weight of Resentment

Resentment is a mental and emotional knot tied to a sense of injustice. It thrives on the belief: *They wronged me, and I cannot let it go.* The ego feeds on this story, replaying the event over and over as though keeping the memory alive will somehow bring resolution.

But resentment does not punish the person who hurt you—it punishes you. It keeps you tethered to the past, reliving the pain and anger as though the event were happening again. Each time you revisit the grievance, you reinforce its presence in your mind and body, creating a cycle of suffering that blocks your ability to experience peace.

Resentment is a thief. It steals your energy, your joy, and your ability to be fully present. The longer you hold onto it, the more it distorts your perspective, narrowing your world to the story of your grievance. To let go of resentment is not to condone what happened; it is to free yourself from its grip, reclaiming the space in your mind and heart that it has occupied for far too long.

The Chains of Guilt

Guilt is the voice of the past, whispering, "You should have done better. You failed. You are not enough." It anchors you to what cannot be changed, turning a momentary mistake into a permanent identity. The ego uses guilt to keep you focused on your shortcomings, convincing you that self-punishment is the path to redemption.

But guilt does not change the past. It does not undo what has been done or make you a better person. Instead, it weighs you down, clouding your ability to grow, learn, and move forward. Guilt becomes a cage, keeping you trapped in self-judgment and shame, unable to see the possibilities that exist in the present.

When you hold onto guilt, you deny yourself the grace of being human. To let go of guilt is not to excuse your actions but to recognize that growth comes from awareness, not self-condemnation. It is to accept that you are more than your mistakes and that the present moment holds the power to create something new.

The Paralysis of Fear

Fear, unlike resentment and guilt, is often tied to the future. It whispers: *Something bad will happen. You won't be able to handle it.* The ego amplifies this fear, conjuring scenarios that feel so real that you react as though they are already happening.

Fear serves a purpose in moments of genuine danger, but the fear the ego perpetuates is often misplaced. It is not rooted in the reality of the present but in the stories of the mind. This fear keeps you stuck, paralyzed by what might happen, unable to take the steps that would lead to growth or change.

The cost of holding onto fear is profound. It limits your actions, narrows your perspective, and prevents you from fully engaging with life. When you cling to fear, you live in a state of contraction, avoiding risk and uncertainty at the expense of freedom and possibility.

To release fear is to step into trust—not trust that nothing bad will ever happen, but trust that you have the strength to face whatever arises. It is to see fear for what it is: a thought, not a reality.

The Consequences of Holding On

Clinging to resentment, guilt, or fear comes at a high cost:

Loss of Presence: These emotions pull your attention away from the present moment, binding you to the past or projecting you into the future. In doing so, they rob you of the peace and vitality that are only available now.

Emotional Exhaustion: Holding onto these emotions requires energy. The constant mental replay of grievances, mistakes, or fears drains your vitality, leaving you feeling depleted and stuck.

Distorted Perception: Resentment, guilt, and fear color your view of life, relationships, and yourself. They narrow your perspective, creating a reality shaped by pain and limitation rather than possibility and freedom.

Blocked Growth: These emotions keep you rooted in old patterns, preventing you from evolving. Growth requires letting go of what no longer serves you, but holding on keeps you tethered to the very things that hold you back.

Letting Go as Liberation

Letting go of resentment, guilt, and fear is not easy because the ego clings to them as part of its identity. It fears that releasing them will leave a void, a loss of the familiar, even if the familiar is painful. But in truth, letting go does not diminish you; it frees you. It creates space for peace, clarity, and renewal to arise.

To let go is not to forget, condone, or suppress. It is to release the grip of these emotions and allow them to flow through you rather than define you. It is to see them for what they are—temporary experiences, not permanent truths.

A Reflection

Ask yourself:

What resentment am I holding onto? What would it feel like to release it, even for a moment?

What guilt continues to weigh me down? Can I see it as a lesson rather than a life sentence?

What fear keeps me from moving forward? What would it feel like to trust myself instead of the stories of my mind?

Freedom begins when you recognize the cost of holding on and choose to let go. In that letting go, you do not lose yourself; you rediscover the self that has always been free, beneath the weight of what you have carried.

Reflect: What Are You Trading for This Attachment?

Every attachment—whether it is to resentment, guilt, fear, or even an identity—comes with a cost. To hold on is to exchange something valuable for something that ultimately burdens you. The question is not only *Why am I holding onto this?* But also, *What am I trading in order to keep it?*

When you hold on to resentment, guilt, or fear, you trade something valuable in exchange. Peace, freedom, and joy are often the first casualties. Take a moment to reflect: What are you sacrificing for these attachments? And is the trade worth it?

Take a moment to reflect:

Resentment: What am I trading to keep this

resentment alive?

> Am I trading peace for anger, harmony for division, or the potential for healing in exchange for the comfort of my grievance?

> Does holding onto this resentment make me feel more in control, or is it controlling me?

Guilt: What am I sacrificing by clinging to guilt?

> Am I trading freedom for self-punishment or the opportunity to grow for a fixation on the past?

> Is this guilt teaching me something valuable, or is it keeping me stuck in shame and regret?

Fear: What possibilities am I giving up by holding onto fear?

> Am I trading the joy of the present moment for anxiety about a future that may never come?

> Is this fear protecting me, or is it paralyzing me, keeping me from fully living?

Identity: What is my attachment to this role or story costing me?

> Am I trading authenticity for the comfort of the familiar?

> Is this identity empowering me, or is it limiting my potential for growth and change?

An Invitation to Awareness

With each attachment, ask yourself:

What am I holding onto, and why?

What am I giving up in order to keep this attachment alive?

Is this trade worth it?

When you honestly reflect on what you are trading, you may realize that the cost of holding on far outweighs the perceived benefit. You may see that what you are clinging to is not serving you—it is consuming you.

The Freedom of Letting Go

Letting go does not mean losing something; it means reclaiming what you have been trading away. It means rediscovering peace, freedom, and joy—the treasures that have always been yours but have been overshadowed by the weight of what you carry.

Ask yourself:

What would my life feel like if I stopped making this trade?

Sit with this question, and let the answer guide you toward the freedom that lies in letting go.

Part Three: Moving Beyond

Chapter Seven

The Power of Presence

"Be where you are; otherwise, you will miss your life."

— Buddha

To be present is to step fully into life as it is unfolding, unfiltered by the mind's stories, unburdened by the past, and unclouded by fears of the future. Presence is not something you acquire or create; it is already here, always available, waiting for your attention. The present moment is the only reality, yet so few of us truly live in it. We spend much of our lives consumed by thoughts about what has been or what might be, missing the richness and aliveness of what *is*.

The power of presence lies in its simplicity. It is not a destination or an achievement but a state of being. When you are present, you are free—from the burdens of the past, from the anxieties of the future, and from the illusions of the mind. Presence connects you to life in its purest form, revealing the depth, beauty, and peace that are always here beneath the noise of thought.

Why the Now Is All There Is

The mind resists the now because it cannot control it. The past and future are the mind's playground, places where it can weave stories, analyze, and predict. But the now is beyond the mind's grasp. It is not a concept or a thought; it is a direct experience.

The past exists only as a memory, a story in your mind. The future exists only as a projection, an imagined possibility. Both are mental constructs. The present moment, however, is real. It is the space where life happens. Every thought, every emotion, every experience arises in the now. Even when you think about the past or future, you are doing so in the present moment.

When you truly understand this, you see that life is not something that happened yesterday or will happen tomorrow. Life is happening now. To be present is to align yourself with reality, to step out of the mental abstractions that create suffering and into the immediacy of being.

The Mind's Resistance to Presence

The mind resists presence because it fears its own irrelevance. In the stillness of the now, the mind's stories lose their power. The ego, which is built on identification with past and future, begins to dissolve. This is why the mind constantly pulls you away from the present, distracting you with thoughts of what was or what might be.

The mind says:

If I dwell on the past, I can make sense of it.

If I worry about the future, I can control it.

If I think enough, I can solve everything.

But these are illusions. The past cannot be changed, the future cannot be controlled, and thinking alone cannot bring peace. Presence, on the other hand, requires no effort, no striving. It is a state of being, not doing.

The Stillness of Presence

Presence is not just about what you do; it is about how you are. It is the stillness beneath the activity of life, the quiet awareness that observes without judgment. When you are present, you are not caught up in the mental noise of "should" or "shouldn't." You are simply here, fully alive in the moment.

Imagine standing by a calm lake. The surface of the water is still, reflecting the sky above. This stillness is presence. Now imagine throwing a stone into the lake. Ripples form, distorting the reflection. The ripples are like the activity of the mind—thoughts, judgments, and stories. But beneath the surface, the lake remains undisturbed. Presence is the awareness that lies beneath the ripples of thought, always still, always clear.

The Gifts of Presence

When you are present, you open yourself to the gifts of the now:

> **Peace:** In presence, you are free from the mind's chatter. You are no longer resisting what is or clinging to what was. This creates a profound sense of peace.

> **Clarity:** Presence allows you to see life as it is rather than through the lens of past experiences or future fears. You respond to life with wisdom, not reactivity.

Connection: In presence, you are fully engaged with the world around you. You experience relationships, nature, and even mundane moments with depth and intimacy.

Freedom: Presence liberates you from the ego's grip. You are no longer bound by roles, labels, or stories. You are simply here, free to be.

Presence Is Not Passive

To be present does not mean to abandon action or responsibility. Presence is not passivity; it is the foundation for authentic and effective action. When you act from presence, you act with clarity and intention rather than from fear or compulsion. Your actions are aligned with the reality of the moment, not driven by mental projections or resistance.

For example:

When you are present, you listen deeply without formulating your response in advance.

When you are present, you work with focus and ease, unburdened by distractions or stress.

When you are present, you meet challenges with equanimity, responding to them as they are, not as the mind imagines them to be.

Presence brings a sense of flow to your life. It connects you to the natural rhythm of existence, where effortlessness replaces struggle and grace replaces resistance.

How to Enter Presence

Presence is not something you achieve; it is something you allow. It begins with a shift in attention—from the mind's stories to the reality of this moment. Here are a few ways to step into presence:

1. **Notice Your Breath:** Bring your attention to the sensation of breathing. Feel the air entering and leaving your body. This simple act anchors you in the now.

2. **Observe Your Surroundings:** Look around without labeling or judging. Notice the colors, shapes, and textures. Be fully present with what you see.

3. **Feel Your Body:** Tune into the sensations in your body—the weight of your feet on the ground, the movement of your hands, the beating of your heart. These sensations bring you into direct contact with the present moment.

Each time you bring your attention to the now, you weaken the pull of the mind and strengthen your connection to presence.

Living in the Now

To live in the now is to live in alignment with life. It is to let go of the mental resistance that creates suffering and to embrace the flow of existence as it unfolds. The power of presence is not something outside of you; it is the essence of who you are. When you stop seeking it and simply allow it, you discover that the now has always been enough.

Ask yourself: *What is here in this moment, beneath the noise of thought?* Pause and listen. The answer is not something you think—it is something you feel, something you know without words. It is presence itself, the silent power that holds all of life.

The Freedom That Arises When We Stop Identifying with the Mind's Chatter

The mind is a constant stream of chatter—a relentless

narrator that comments, analyzes, judges, and replays. It creates an endless loop of thoughts, often disconnected from the reality of the present moment. This chatter is so pervasive that we mistake it for who we are. But the truth is, you are not your thoughts. You are the awareness in which those thoughts arise and dissolve.

When you stop identifying with the mind's chatter, a profound freedom emerges—a freedom from the weight of the past, the fear of the future, and the mental noise that keeps you tethered to suffering. In this freedom, you discover peace, clarity, and the spaciousness of your true self.

The Illusion of Identification

Identification with the mind's chatter is the root of much of our suffering. The thoughts in your mind often reflect fear, judgment, and attachment, creating a narrative about who you are and what your life is. When you identify with these thoughts, you become entangled in their stories, believing them to be the ultimate truth.

For example:

A thought arises: *I'm not good enough.* When you identify with this thought, it becomes more than a passing mental event; it becomes a belief about your worth. You carry it with you, allowing it to shape your actions and perceptions.

Another thought appears: *They don't respect me.* Identified with this thought, you react with anger or defensiveness, creating conflict in your relationships.

Or perhaps the mind whispers: *What if something*

bad happens? You mistake this projection for reality, allowing fear to paralyze you.

This identification is the ego at work. The ego thrives on mental noise because it reinforces the illusion of a separate self—a self defined by its stories, roles, and fears. To stop identifying with the mind's chatter is to step out of the ego's grasp and into the spaciousness of awareness.

What Happens When You Stop Identifying

When you stop identifying with the mind's chatter, a profound shift occurs. Thoughts may still arise, but they no longer define you. Instead of being lost in the stories of the mind, you become the observer—the silent presence that watches thoughts come and go.

Thoughts Lose Their Power. Without identification, thoughts no longer have the power to control your emotions or actions. A thought like *I'm not good enough* is seen for what it is—a passing mental event, not a truth. You notice it, but it doesn't anchor itself in your sense of self.

You Access Inner Stillness. The chatter of the mind can feel like a storm, loud and overwhelming. When you stop identifying with it, you find the stillness beneath the storm. This stillness is not something you create; it is always there, waiting to be noticed. In this stillness, you experience a deep peace that is not dependent on external circumstances.

You Respond Instead of React. Identification with thoughts often leads to reactive behavior. But when you are no longer entangled in the mind's chatter, you create space between stimulus and response. This space allows you to act with clarity and intention rather than from unconscious patterns.

You Reconnect with the Present Moment. The mind's chatter pulls you away from the now, dragging you into the past or projecting you into the future. Without identification, you return to the present moment, the only place where life truly happens. In this presence, you find freedom from the mind's distortions.

The Nature of Freedom

The freedom that arises when you stop identifying with the mind's chatter is not a freedom the mind can understand. It is not the freedom to do whatever you want or to control life. It is the freedom to be—to exist fully and authentically in the reality of this moment, unburdened by the noise of thought.

This freedom is spacious. It feels like stepping out of a confined room into an open field. The walls of thought and identity dissolve, and you realize that you were never trapped except by your own identification with the mind.

This freedom is light. It lifts the heaviness of fear, judgment, and attachment, allowing you to move through life with ease. You are no longer carrying the weight of every thought, every story, every mental projection.

This freedom is liberating. It is the realization that you are not bound by the mind's chatter. You are the awareness in which the chatter arises, a vast and infinite presence that cannot be defined or limited.

How to Dis-identify from the Mind

Dis-identification does not mean suppressing or fighting your thoughts. It means observing them with awareness and allowing them to come and go without attaching to them. Here are practical steps to help you dis-identify from the mind's chatter:

> **1. Become the Observer.** The next time a thought arises, pause and notice it. Say to yourself: *Ah, there's a thought.* Recognize that you are the one observing the thought, not the thought itself.

> **2. Label the Chatter.** When the mind starts to spiral into chatter, label it gently: *This is fear,* or *This is judgment.* Labeling creates distance, helping you see the chatter as separate from your true self.

> **3. Shift Your Attention.** Bring your attention to something real and tangible in the present moment—your breath, the sensation of your body, or the sounds around you. This anchors you in awareness and weakens the pull of thought.

> **4. Ask, "Who Am I Without This Thought?"** When a persistent thought arises, ask yourself: *Who am I without this thought?* This question can reveal the space of awareness beyond the chatter, where your true self resides.

Living Beyond the Mind

To live beyond the mind's chatter is not to eliminate thought but to transcend identification with it. Thoughts may arise, but they no longer define you. You experience them as ripples on the surface of a vast ocean—dynamic but impermanent, unable to disturb the depth of your being.

Ask yourself:

What would it feel like to simply observe my thoughts without believing or resisting them?

Who am I beyond the stories my mind tells?

In the freedom that arises, you find yourself no longer tethered to the noise of the mind. You step into the spaciousness of presence, where life flows freely, and your true essence shines unobscured. This is the power of dis-identification—the gateway to peace, clarity, and liberation.

Mindfulness: Practicing Presence in Everyday Life

Mindfulness is the art of bringing your full attention to the present moment. It is a practice of presence, a way of aligning your awareness with the here and now. While presence is your natural state, the mind's tendency to wander into thoughts of the past and future often pulls you away from it. Mindfulness serves as a bridge, helping you return to the immediacy of life and experience it fully.

Mindfulness is not about doing more; it is about being fully where you are. Whether you are washing dishes, walking, or speaking with a loved one, mindfulness invites you to bring your whole self to the experience. It transforms ordinary moments into opportunities for presence, connection, and peace.

What Is Mindfulness?

Mindfulness is the practice of paying attention to the present moment intentionally and without judgment. It involves noticing what is happening around you and within you—your thoughts, emotions, bodily sensations, and environment—without becoming entangled in them.

Mindfulness is not about controlling your thoughts or forcing yourself to stay in the moment. It is about observing your experience as it is, with openness and curiosity. In doing so, mindfulness becomes a powerful tool for practicing presence, grounding you in the reality of what is rather than the mental noise of what was or what might be.

How Mindfulness Cultivates Presence

Anchoring Awareness in the Now

Mindfulness brings your attention to the present moment, interrupting the mind's tendency to drift into the past or future. By focusing on simple, tangible experiences—like the sensation of your breath or the feeling of your feet on the ground—you ground yourself in the now.

Observing Without Judgment

Mindfulness trains you to observe thoughts and emotions without labeling them as good or bad. This non-judgmental awareness creates space between you and your mental chatter, allowing you to see thoughts and emotions as passing events rather than permanent truths.

Engaging Fully with Life

When you are mindful, you engage fully with whatever you are doing, no matter how mundane. Washing dishes becomes an opportunity to feel the warmth of the water, the texture of the soap bubbles, and the rhythm of your movements. Walking becomes a practice of feeling the earth beneath your feet and noticing the world around you. Each moment becomes an invitation to experience life directly rather than through the filter of thought.

Mindfulness in Everyday Life

Mindfulness is not confined to formal meditation. It is a way of living, a practice that can be woven into the fabric of your daily life. Here are some simple ways to bring mindfulness into your everyday moments:

Mindful Breathing. Throughout the day, take a moment to focus on your breath. Notice the sensation of the air entering and leaving your body. This simple act brings you into the present and calms the mind.

Mindful Eating. When you eat, slow down. Notice the colors, textures, and flavors of your food. Chew slowly, paying attention to each bite. Eating mindfully transforms a routine activity into a rich sensory experience.

Mindful Walking. Whether you're walking to your car or taking a stroll in nature, bring your attention to the act of walking. Feel the movement of your body, the sensation of your feet touching the ground, and the rhythm of your steps.

Mindful Listening. In conversations, listen deeply without planning your response or getting lost in your own thoughts. Give your full attention to the person speaking, noticing their words, tone, and energy. This creates a deeper connection and presence in your relationships.

Mindful Tasks. Whatever task you are doing—washing dishes, folding laundry, or typing an email—do it with full attention. Notice the details of the activity, the movements of your body, and the sensations involved. Let the task be your anchor to the   now.

The Benefits of Mindfulness

Practicing mindfulness cultivates presence, which has far-reaching benefits for your well-being and your experience of life:

> **Reduces Stress:** By grounding you in the present, mindfulness helps you step out of the cycle of worry and overthinking that fuels stress.

> **Enhances Clarity:** Mindfulness clears mental clutter, allowing you to see situations more objectively and respond with wisdom rather than reactivity.

> **Improves Relationships:** When you are fully present with others, you create deeper connections, foster understanding, and communicate with authenticity.

> **Increases Joy:** Mindfulness opens your awareness to the beauty of life's simple moments, helping you find joy and gratitude in the here and now.

Mindfulness and the Ego

Mindfulness is also a way to step out of the ego's grip. The ego thrives on distraction, keeping you focused on past regrets or future fears. Mindfulness disrupts this pattern by bringing your attention to the present, where the ego has no foothold. In mindfulness, you experience life directly, free from the ego's filters and distortions.

A Reflection

Ask yourself:

> *How often am I fully present in my daily life? What moments tend to pull me out of the now?*
>
> *What would it feel like to give my full attention to one simple activity today—whether it's eating, walking, or listening?*
>
> *What small steps can I take to cultivate mindfulness in my everyday routines?*

Mindfulness is not about achieving perfection. It is about returning, again and again, to the present moment. Each time you practice mindfulness, you strengthen your connection to presence and deepen your experience of life. In this way, mindfulness becomes a pathway to freedom—a way to live fully and freely, one moment at a time.

Chapter Eight

Surrender as a Radical Act of Acceptance

"Acceptance doesn't mean resignation; it means understanding that something is what it is and that there's got to be a way through it."

— Michael J. Fox

Surrender is often misunderstood. It is not about giving up or resigning yourself to circumstances. It is not a sign of weakness or passivity. True surrender is a radical act of acceptance—a willingness to let life be as it is without resistance or judgment. Surrender is not the end of your power but the beginning of a deeper, more profound strength.

When you surrender, you stop fighting what cannot be changed. You release the illusion of control and align yourself with the flow of life. This alignment does not mean you lose your ability to act or respond; it means your actions arise from clarity and peace rather than resistance or fear. Surrender is the bridge between suffering and freedom, a gateway to living fully in the present moment.

What Does It Mean to Surrender?

To surrender is to accept what is. It is to stop mentally resisting life's unfolding and instead meet it with openness and presence. Surrender does not mean you approve of or like everything that happens. It means you stop arguing with reality and accept it as it is, not as you wish it to be.

Surrender is not passive. It does not mean you do nothing in the face of difficulty or injustice. Instead, surrender is about dropping the inner struggle—the mental and emotional resistance that amplifies suffering. You can respond to life with greater wisdom, strength, and effectiveness from this state of acceptance.

For example:

> If you are facing a challenge, surrender does not mean ignoring it or giving up. It means accepting the reality of the challenge without resistance so you can address it with a clear and focused mind.

> If you are experiencing pain, surrender does not mean denying it or pretending it doesn't exist. It means allowing yourself to fully feel the pain without adding layers of mental resistance like *This shouldn't be happening* or *Why me?*

The Ego's Resistance to Surrender

The ego fears surrender because it interprets acceptance as defeat. It thrives on resistance, control, and struggle—it believes that to let go is to lose. The ego clings to the idea that life must conform to its expectations, and when it doesn't, it fights against reality.

The ego says:

If I surrender, I will lose control.

If I accept this, it means I'm weak.

If I let go, I'll stop trying, and everything will fall apart.

But these fears are illusions. Surrender does not weaken you; it frees you from the mental and emotional turmoil of resistance. The control the ego seeks is an illusion, and clinging to it only deepens your suffering. True power arises not from resistance but from alignment with the reality of the present moment.

Surrender as Freedom

When you surrender, you free yourself from the inner battle with life. Resistance creates tension, stress, and suffering, while surrender dissolves these burdens. In surrender, you discover a profound sense of peace—not because your circumstances have changed, but because your relationship to them has shifted.

Surrender liberates you from the need to control everything. It allows you to trust the flow of life and to see that you do not need to force or manipulate outcomes to find peace. This trust opens the door to freedom:

Freedom from Resistance: By accepting what is, you stop adding layers of suffering to your experience.

Freedom from Fear: Surrender helps you see that fear is often a projection of the mind, not a reflection of reality. In accepting the moment, fear loses its grip.

Freedom from the Ego: Surrender dissolves the ego's illusions of control and separateness, connecting you to the deeper truth of your being.

The Power of Acceptance

Acceptance is at the heart of surrender. When you accept life as it is, you no longer waste energy resisting or denying reality. This does not mean you condone everything that happens; it means you recognize that resistance will not change what has already occurred. Acceptance allows you to meet life as it is, freeing you to respond rather than react.

For example:

> When faced with a loss, acceptance allows you to grieve fully without resisting the pain. This openness to your experience creates space for healing.

> When faced with uncertainty, acceptance allows you to let go of the need for control and trust in the unfolding of life.

> When faced with conflict, acceptance allows you to drop your defenses and approach the situation with clarity and compassion.

Acceptance is not about passivity; it is about presence. *It is the recognition that this moment is as it is*, and in that recognition, you find the strength to act wisely and authentically.

Surrender and the Present Moment

Surrender anchors you in the present moment. Resistance keeps you trapped in the past or projected into the future, replaying what has already happened or worrying about what might come. Surrender brings you back to now, the only place where life is happening.

In the present moment, there is no room for resistance because there is nothing to resist. The past is gone, the future is not here, and this moment is. To surrender is to embrace the now fully, to allow it to unfold without interference or judgment.

Practical Steps Toward Surrender

Surrender is not a single act but an ongoing practice. It requires awareness, patience, and a willingness to let go of the mind's need for control. Here are some steps to help you cultivate surrender:

1. Notice Resistance. Pay attention to moments when you feel resistance—whether it's a thought like *This shouldn't be happening* or a feeling of tension in your body. Simply notice the resistance without judgment.

2. Name the Reality. Acknowledge what is happening in the moment. For example: *I feel sadness,* or *This situation is difficult.* Naming reality helps you accept it rather than resist it.

3. Release Judgment. Let go of labeling the situation as good or bad. Instead, allow it to be as it is. Remember, acceptance does not mean approval; it means recognizing reality without adding mental resistance.

4. Focus on the Now. Bring your attention to the present moment. Notice your breath, the sensations in your body, or the sounds around you. This anchors you in presence and helps dissolve resistance.

5. Trust Life. Remind yourself that surrender is not giving up; it is aligning with the flow of life. Trust that life is unfolding as it must, even if you cannot see the bigger picture.

A Reflection

Ask yourself:

What am I resisting in my life right now? How does

this resistance feel in my mind and body?

What would it feel like to accept this moment as it is, even if I don't like it?

What might I gain by surrendering to what is, rather than fighting against it?

In surrender, you do not lose control; you release the illusion of control. You stop resisting life and instead flow with it, discovering a peace and freedom that cannot be found through struggle. Surrender is not a passive act—it is the most radical, transformative act of acceptance. Through surrender, you align with the deeper intelligence of life and discover the profound power of simply being.

The Difference Between Passive Resignation and Active Surrender

At first glance, surrender might seem similar to resignation. Both involve a sense of letting go, of ceasing resistance. However, the two are fundamentally different in their energy, intention, and outcome. *Passive resignation* is rooted in defeat, apathy, or powerlessness, while *active surrender* is a conscious and empowered choice to align with reality and flow with life. Understanding this difference is essential for cultivating true surrender, which leads not to stagnation but to freedom and clarity.

Passive Resignation: Giving Up

Passive resignation is the act of mentally and emotionally giving up. It stems from a place of defeat, where you perceive yourself as powerless to influence your circumstances. It is often accompanied by feelings of victimhood, hopelessness, and apathy. Resignation has an energy of heaviness and stagnation, where you feel stuck and disconnected from life.

In resignation, there is no acceptance of what is. Instead, there is a sense of resistance disguised as withdrawal. You may think or say:

There's no point in trying.

This is just the way things are, and nothing can be done.

I have no choice but to endure this.

Resignation leads to inaction and often deepens suffering because it perpetuates a sense of separation from life. It does not bring peace but instead leaves you feeling disconnected, disempowered, and resigned to a reality you believe you cannot change.

Active Surrender: Letting Go

Active surrender, in contrast, is a powerful act of acceptance. It is not about giving up but about letting go of the mental and emotional resistance that keeps you stuck. Surrender involves consciously choosing to accept reality as it is, without judgment or attachment. It is an active alignment with the present moment, rooted in trust, awareness, and openness.

In surrender, there is no sense of defeat but rather a sense of liberation. You are not withdrawing from life; you are stepping fully into it, allowing life to unfold without trying to control or resist it. Surrender might involve thoughts like:

This is what is happening now, and I accept it.

I cannot change this situation, but I can choose how I respond.

By letting go, I create space for peace and clarity.

Active surrender brings freedom, peace, and connection

because it allows you to flow with life rather than against it. It is not a passive state but a deeply intentional one, requiring awareness, courage, and trust.

Key Differences Between Resignation and Surrender

Aspect	Passive Resignation	Active Surrender
Energy	Heavy, stagnant, apathetic	Light, liberating, intentional
Rooted In	Defeat, hopelessness, victimhood	Acceptance, trust, awareness
Response to Reality	Withdraws, avoids, or gives up	Aligns, engages, and flows
Outcome	Stagnation, disconnection, continued suffering	Freedom, peace, clarity, and empowerment
Perspective	*Life is happening to me.*	*Life is happening for me, and I trust its flow*

Examples of Passive Resignation vs. Active Surrender

A Challenging Relationship

Resignation: You withdraw emotionally and stop communicating, thinking: *This relationship is broken, and there's nothing I can do to fix it.*

Surrender: You accept the reality of the relationship as it is. You stop trying to force change but remain present, open to communication, and aligned with your own values. Think: *This is where the relationship is right now. I will engage with honesty and let the outcome unfold.*

A Job Loss

Resignation: You feel defeated and paralyzed, thinking: This is the end of my career. There's no point in trying anymore.

Surrender: You acknowledge the reality of the situation and trust that this challenge may open new doors, thinking: *This has happened, and while it's difficult, I will take the next step and see where life leads.*

Physical Illness or Pain

Resignation: You see yourself as a victim of your condition, thinking: *Why me? There's no point in trying to live fully anymore.*

Surrender: You accept the reality of your condition and focus on what you can do to live with grace, thinking: *This is the body I have right now. I will care for it and make the most of each moment.*

Why Passive Resignation Creates Suffering

Resignation creates suffering because it disconnects you from the flow of life. By withdrawing, you separate yourself from your own power to engage with the present moment. Resignation keeps you stuck in resistance, even as it appears to be an act of letting go. This resistance may be subtle—a sense of hopelessness or self-pity—but it perpetuates the mental and emotional struggle.

Why Active Surrender Brings Freedom

Active surrender brings freedom because it dissolves resistance. When you stop fighting what is, you free yourself from the tension and stress of trying to control the uncontrollable. Surrender allows you to meet life as it is, opening the door to new possibilities and insights. It does not mean you abandon effort; it means your efforts are no longer driven by fear, resistance, or attachment.

Surrender connects you to the deeper intelligence of life. It aligns you with the natural flow, where clarity replaces confusion and peace replaces struggle. In surrender, you discover that life is not something to be fought against but something to be lived fully, with presence and trust.

How to Shift from Resignation to Surrender

Cultivate Awareness. Notice when you feel heavy, stuck, or disconnected. Ask yourself: Am I resisting reality or withdrawing from it?

Acknowledge Reality. Acceptance begins with acknowledgment. Name the situation as it is without judgment. For example: This is happening right now.

Release Judgment. Let go of thoughts like This shouldn't be happening. Accept that reality is as it is, even if it is difficult or unpleasant.

Engage with Presence. Instead of withdrawing, bring your full presence to the moment. Ask: What can I do now, from a place of clarity and alignment?

Trust the Process. Remind yourself that surrender is not the end of your power but the beginning of true alignment with life. Trust that by letting go, you create space for peace and possibility.

A Reflection

Ask yourself:

Where in my life am I practicing resignation instead of surrender?

What would it feel like to release resistance and fully accept what is, while staying present and engaged?

How might surrender open the door to freedom and clarity in this situation?

Surrender teaches you to accept life as it is. But what about the uncertainty of what's to come? To live fully, you must also embrace the unknown, trusting life's unfolding without needing to control it.

We'd Love to Hear From You!

Thank you so much for reading this book-it means the world to me. If you found it helpful, inspiring, or just enjoyable, would you take a moment to leave a review? Your feedback not only helps others but also keeps me motivated to create more valuable content for you.

Here's how you can leave a review:

1. Scan the QR code on this page to go directly to the Author's page.

2. Or, visit your Amazon Orders page, find this book, and click "Write a Product Review."

Your kind words make a big difference.
Thank you for your support!

Chapter Nine

Embracing the Unknown

"The only thing that makes life possible is permanent, intolerable uncertainty; not knowing what comes next."

— Ursula K. Le Guin

Letting Go of the Fear of the Future

Fear of the future is one of the most pervasive forms of suffering. It arises from the mind's need for certainty, its relentless attempt to predict and control what has not yet happened. The irony is that this fear, which is entirely focused on the future, is deeply rooted in the past. The mind takes memories of past pain, failure, or disappointment and projects them forward, creating a narrative of what *might* happen. Doing so binds you to both the past and the future, pulling you away from the only place where life truly exists: the present moment.

To embrace the unknown is to release this fear. It is to step out of the mind's stories and into the flow of life, trusting that the present moment will always provide what you need. Embracing the unknown does not mean abandoning responsibility or foresight; it means letting go of the illusion that the future can be controlled through worry or resistance.

The Mind's Fear of the Future

The mind resists uncertainty because it sees the unknown as a threat. It operates under the belief: *If I can predict what will happen, I can protect myself.* However, this belief is flawed because the future is inherently unknowable. No amount of mental effort can eliminate its uncertainty.

The fear of the future manifests as anxiety, worry, and overthinking. The mind becomes consumed with "what if" scenarios:

> *What if I fail?*

> *What if I lose what I have?*

> *What if I make the wrong choice?*

Each question is rooted in a deeper fear of reliving past pain. The mind remembers experiences of failure, loss, or hardship and assumes that these must repeat in the future. It projects the past forward, creating an endless cycle of fear and resistance.

How Fear of the Future Ties Us to the Past

The mind uses the past as a blueprint for the future. It recalls moments of difficulty and says: *This is what happened before, and it could happen again.* In this way, fear of the future is not about the future at all—it is about the mind's inability to let go of the past.

For example:

> If you were betrayed in a relationship, the mind might say: *I must protect myself from being hurt again.* This fear keeps you guarded and

mistrustful, even in new relationships.

If you experienced failure in your career, the mind might say: *What if I fail again?* This fear holds you back from taking risks or pursuing new opportunities.

By clinging to the past, the mind creates a self-fulfilling prophecy. It blinds you to the possibilities of the present moment, limiting your ability to step into the unknown with openness and trust.

The Freedom of Embracing the Unknown

To embrace the unknown is to release the grip of the past and step fully into the present. It is to recognize that the future does not exist as a reality—it exists only as a mental projection. The only reality is now, and in this moment, there is nothing to fear.

When you embrace the unknown, you no longer need to predict or control what will happen. Instead, you trust yourself to meet life as it unfolds. This trust is not based on external circumstances but on the deeper knowing that you are always equipped to navigate whatever arises. You begin to see uncertainty not as a threat but as a space of infinite possibility.

Why the Mind Fears Letting Go

The mind resists embracing the unknown because it equates uncertainty with danger. It clings to the familiar, even if the familiar is painful because it feels safer than stepping into the unknown. The mind says:

At least I know what to expect from the past.

If I let go, I might lose control.

But this is an illusion. The mind never truly has control; it only has the illusion of control. Life unfolds in unpredictable ways, and clinging to the past only creates tension and suffering. Letting go of this need for control is not a loss—it is a liberation.

The Present Moment as the Gateway to Freedom

Life happens only in the present moment, yet fear of the future can distract you. When you worry about what might happen, you miss the richness of what is happening now. Embracing the unknown means anchoring yourself in the now, allowing the future to unfold naturally without mental interference.

Ask yourself:

What is here in this moment?

Am I experiencing real danger, or is my fear a projection of the mind?

What would it feel like to simply trust this moment as it is?

You break free from the mind's grip on the future by bringing your attention back to the now. You discover that the present moment holds everything you need—clarity, peace, and the ability to respond to life as it arises.

Living with Openness and Trust

Embracing the unknown is not about ignoring the future; it is about trusting life. It is about recognizing that uncertainty is not something to be feared but something to be welcomed. The unknown is where growth happens, where possibilities arise, and where life unfolds in its fullness.

To live with openness and trust, you must let go of the mind's need for guarantees. This does not mean you abandon planning or preparation; it means you approach life with a sense of curiosity rather than fear. You say:

> *I do not know what will happen, but I trust myself to navigate it.*

> *I release the past and open myself to the infinite possibilities of the now.*

A Reflection

Ask yourself:

> *What fears do I have about the future? Are these fears based on reality, or are they projections of the past?*

> *What would it feel like to embrace uncertainty rather than resist it?*

> *How might my life change if I trusted the present moment instead of fearing the future?*

Embracing the unknown is not an act of passivity; it is an act of courage. It is a willingness to step into life without the safety net of certainty, trusting that you are always supported by the present moment. In this trust, you find freedom—not freedom from uncertainty, but freedom within it. You discover that the unknown is not your enemy; it is the space where life's greatest possibilities await.

The Unknown as a Space of Infinite Potential

The unknown is often perceived as a void—an absence of certainty, control, or familiarity. The mind, conditioned to seek security, tends to fear this void, interpreting it as a place of chaos or danger. But the unknown is not a void to be feared; it is a space of infinite potential. It is the fertile ground from which all things arise, the source of creativity, transformation, and growth.

To philosophically frame the unknown as infinite potential is to shift your perspective from fear to wonder. It is to see the unknown not as an obstacle but as an invitation, a space where possibilities exist beyond the limits of your imagination. In the unknown, the future is unwritten, and life is free to unfold in ways you cannot predict or control. This freedom, while unsettling to the mind, is also the essence of its beauty.

The Mind's Fear of the Unknown

The mind fears the unknown because it cannot define or control it. The mind operates within the boundaries of the known—what has already been experienced, labeled, and understood. The unknown, by its very nature, exists outside these boundaries, defying the mind's need for certainty and structure.

This fear arises from the mind's attachment to the past. It says:

> *If I do not know what will happen, I cannot prepare.*

> *If I step into the unknown, I might lose what I have or who I am.*

> *The unknown is dangerous because it is unpredictable.*

But these fears are illusions created by the mind. The unknown itself is neither dangerous nor safe; it simply is. The mind projects its own insecurities onto the unknown, filling it with imagined threats. In reality, the unknown is neutral—it is a blank canvas upon which life paints its masterpiece.

The Unknown as Infinite Possibility

When you release the mind's fear and resistance, you begin

to see the unknown for what it truly is: a space of infinite potential. Unlike the known, which is fixed and limited by past experience, the unknown is boundless. It is the realm of creation, where new ideas, opportunities, and ways of being emerge.

Consider this:

> Every discovery, invention, and work of art has arisen from the unknown. Before it existed, it was only a possibility waiting to be realized.

> Every new relationship, experience, or chapter of your life begins in the unknown. The very nature of life is to evolve, to grow, and to expand into what is not yet known.

The unknown is the source of life's dynamism. It is where transformation happens, where the old gives way to the new, and where you are invited to step beyond the limitations of your current understanding. To fear the unknown is to fear life itself, while to embrace it is to align with the infinite creative potential of existence.

The Stillness of Infinite Potential

The unknown is not chaotic or random; it is still and vast, like the depths of the ocean or the expanse of the night sky. In this stillness, everything exists in potential. It is not yet formed, not yet expressed, but it holds within it the seeds of all that can be.

This stillness can be felt when you pause and let go of the mind's activity. When you stop projecting fears or expectations onto the unknown, you experience its spaciousness. In this spaciousness, you find freedom—freedom from the limitations of the past, freedom from the need to control, and freedom to create anew.

The unknown does not demand anything of you; it simply invites you to be present with it. In this presence, you realize that the potential of the unknown is not something outside of you—it is also within you. You are a part of this infinite space, and your awareness is the bridge between what is and what can be.

The Unknown and Trust

To embrace the unknown as infinite potential, you must cultivate trust. Trust is not about knowing what will happen; it is about knowing that you have the capacity to meet whatever arises. It is about trusting the intelligence of life, the flow of existence, and your own inner resourcefulness.

This trust is not blind or naive; it is a deep recognition that life is not static or limited. The same intelligence that creates galaxies, grows forests, and beats your heart is also guiding the unfolding of your life. When you trust the unknown, you align yourself with this intelligence, allowing life to move through you in ways that are often beyond your understanding.

Freedom in the Unknown

The mind seeks security in the known, but true freedom lies in the unknown. In the known, everything is fixed, familiar, and predictable but also confined. There is no space for growth or discovery. In the unknown, by contrast, there is infinite space—space to explore, to evolve, and to create.

When you embrace the unknown, you free yourself from the need for certainty. You let go of the mind's compulsion to plan, predict, and control. Instead, you open yourself to the flow of life, trusting that each moment will reveal itself as it needs to. This freedom is not about abandoning responsibility or foresight; it is about stepping out of the mind's limitations and into the vastness of possibility.

A Reflection

Ask yourself:

What stories does my mind tell me about the unknown? Are these stories based on reality or fear?

How might my life change if I saw the unknown not as a threat but as a space of possibility?

What would it feel like to trust the unknown, to let it unfold without resistance or control?

The unknown is not something to be feared or avoided; it is the essence of life itself. It is the space where growth, transformation, and creation take place. When you embrace the unknown, you step into a world of infinite potential, where each moment holds the possibility of something new, something beautiful, something beyond what you have ever known. To trust the unknown is to trust life—to trust that its unfolding is always guiding you toward your highest potential.

Trusting Life's Unfolding Without Controlling Every Outcome

Control is the mind's way of seeking security. It believes that planning, predicting, and manipulating circumstances can shape life into something safe and predictable. While there is value in thoughtful preparation and responsibility, the desire to control every outcome stems from fear—fear of uncertainty, failure, or loss. This fear can create a constant state of tension as the mind tirelessly tries to impose order on a reality that is inherently dynamic and ever-changing.

To trust life's unfolding is to step out of this cycle of control and into a state of openness. It is to recognize that life is not something you need to dominate or micromanage; it is something you are a part of. Life has its own rhythm, intelligence, and flow, and when you align yourself with this flow, you discover a freedom and peace that cannot be found in control.

Why Do We Try to Control Life?

The urge to control stems from the ego's belief that it is separate from life. The ego sees itself as the director of the story, responsible for ensuring that everything goes according to plan. This belief leads to:

> **Fear of Uncertainty:** The ego resists the unknown because it cannot predict or control it. It says, *If I don't control this, something bad might happen.*

> **Attachment to Outcomes:** The ego ties its sense of worth and identity to specific results, believing that success, happiness, or safety depend on achieving these outcomes.

> **Illusion of Power:** The ego equates control with strength, believing that letting go is a sign of weakness or passivity.

While these tendencies are natural, they create unnecessary stress and suffering. The more you try to control life, the more you resist its natural flow, and the more you disconnect from the present moment.

The Nature of Life's Flow

Life is not static or predictable. It is a living, dynamic process, always unfolding in ways that are often beyond your understanding. Just as a river flows toward the ocean, life moves according to its own rhythm. You can try to dam the river, redirect it, or fight against it, but ultimately, the river will find its way. The same is true of life—it is always unfolding, whether or not you attempt to control it.

This does not mean life is chaotic or random. On the contrary, life has an inherent intelligence. The same intelligence governs nature's cycles, grows forests from tiny seeds, and beats your heart without your conscious effort. When you trust life's unfolding, you align yourself with this intelligence, allowing it to guide you in ways that are often more profound and harmonious than anything the mind could devise.

What Happens When You Stop Controlling Every Outcome

When you let go of the need to control every outcome, you experience a profound shift:

Freedom from Anxiety: The constant effort to control life creates tension and worry. Letting go dissolves this tension, freeing you from the burden of needing to plan and predict everything.

Connection to the Present Moment: Control pulls you out of the now, keeping you fixated on the future. Trusting life brings you back to the present, where you can fully engage with what is happening.

Openness to Possibility: When you stop trying to force specific outcomes, you open yourself to possibilities you may not have considered. Life often unfolds in ways that exceed your expectations when you allow it to.

Inner Peace: Letting go of control creates a sense of peace and ease. You no longer feel the need to fight against life or resist its natural flow.

Trusting Life's Intelligence

Trusting life does not mean abandoning responsibility or effort. It means recognizing the limits of control and allowing life's intelligence to work with you.

Consider this analogy:

A gardener tends the soil, plants the seeds, and waters the plants. These are actions within their control. However, the gardener cannot force the seeds to grow or control the weather. Growth happens according to the natural intelligence of life. Trusting this process does not diminish the gardener's role—it enhances it.

Similarly, in your own life, trust does not mean doing nothing. It means taking action where appropriate while letting go of the need to control what is beyond your influence. It is a partnership with life, where you do your part and trust the rest to unfold as it will.

How to Trust Life's Unfolding

Trusting life's unfolding is a practice that requires awareness, patience, and a willingness to let go of the ego's need for certainty. Here are some steps to help you cultivate this trust:

1. Acknowledge What You Cannot Control. Begin by

identifying the areas of your life where you are trying to control outcomes. Ask yourself: *Is this within my control, or am I resisting something I cannot change?* Recognize that letting go of what you cannot control is not giving up—it is freeing yourself from unnecessary struggle.

2. Take Inspired Action. Trust does not mean inaction. Do what is within your power to influence, but let your actions come from clarity and presence, not fear or desperation. Ask yourself: *Am I acting from a place of trust, or am I trying to force an outcome?*

3. Stay Present. Bring your attention back to the now. When you catch yourself worrying about the future or trying to predict what will happen, gently redirect your focus to the present moment. Ask: *What is needed right now?*

4. Reframe Uncertainty. Instead of seeing uncertainty as a threat, view it as a space of possibility. Remind yourself: *The unknown is where new opportunities and growth arise.* Trust that life often unfolds in ways that are better than you could have planned.

5. Practice Letting Go. When you feel the urge to control, pause and take a deep breath. Say to yourself: *I release the need to control this. I trust that life will unfold as it is meant to.*

A Reflection

Ask yourself:

> *What areas of my life am I trying to control? How does this effort affect my peace and well-being?*

> *What might happen if I released my need to control and trusted life's unfolding instead?*

> *Can I recognize the moments when life has guided me in unexpected and beautiful ways?*

A New Way of Living

To trust life's unfolding is to live in harmony with the flow of existence. It is to release the need for certainty and embrace the beauty of the unknown. In this trust, you discover that life is not something you must fight against or manipulate. It is a dance, and when you stop trying to lead, you find that life moves you with grace and wisdom.

When you let go of control, you do not lose power—you find a deeper, truer power. You align yourself with life's natural intelligence; in that alignment, you discover peace, freedom, and the infinite possibilities of the present moment. Trust life, and it will guide you in ways beyond what the mind could ever imagine.

Freedom in Letting Go

"In the process of letting go, you will lose many things from the past, but you will find yourself."

— Deepak Chopra

Letting go is often misunderstood as a form of loss—a relinquishing of control, attachments, or identities. The mind equates letting go with deprivation, as though releasing something means you will be left with less. But in truth, letting go is not about losing; it is about gaining. It is a profound act of liberation, a way of freeing yourself from the weight of resistance, fear, and clinging. Letting go is not the end of something—it is the beginning of everything.

The journey through presence, surrender, and embracing the unknown leads to this ultimate realization: freedom lies not in holding on but in releasing. It is in letting go of what no longer serves you, what keeps you stuck, and what clouds your vision that you rediscover the spaciousness of life and the essence of who you truly are.

Letting Go as Liberation

When you let go, you step out of the confines of the mind's narratives. You release the need to control outcomes, the attachment to past grievances, and the fear of the unknown. What remains is not emptiness but fullness—an expansive freedom that arises from living in alignment with life as it is.

Consider:

Letting Go of Resistance: When you let go of resistance, you stop fighting against reality. This creates space for peace and clarity, even in the midst of challenges.

Letting Go of Attachment: When you release attachments to specific outcomes, roles, or identities, you free yourself from the limitations they impose. You discover that your true essence is not tied to these external things.

Letting Go of Fear: When you let go of fear, you embrace trust. You stop projecting past pain onto the future and instead open yourself to the infinite possibilities of the now.

Letting go is not about denying your experiences or detaching from life. It is about engaging with life fully, without the chains of resistance or the weight of clinging. It is a way of saying *yes* to life as it is, trusting that in this openness, you will find everything you need.

Letting Go as a Path to Freedom

Freedom is not something you acquire; it is something you uncover. It has always been within you, obscured only by the layers of resistance, attachment, and fear that the mind creates.

Letting go removes these layers, revealing the freedom that is your natural state.

Freedom is not the absence of challenges or uncertainties. It is the ability to meet these with openness and presence, unburdened by the mind's attempts to control or resist. When you let go, you no longer see life as something to be fought against or mastered. You see it as something to be lived—fully, freely, and authentically.

Letting Go Is a Journey

Letting go is not a single act; it is a journey, a practice that unfolds moment by moment. Each time you release a thought, emotion, or attachment that no longer serves you, you take another step toward freedom. Each time you choose presence over distraction, surrender over resistance, and trust over fear, you deepen your connection to life.

This journey is not linear. There will be moments when the mind's old patterns resurface when fear or attachment takes hold. But each of these moments is an opportunity—a chance to return to awareness, to practice letting go again. Over time, the practice becomes natural, and freedom becomes your way of being.

The Power of Trust

At the heart of letting go is trust: trust in life, trust in the present moment, and trust in yourself. Letting go requires you to release the illusion of control and step into the unknown with faith. This trust is not blind or naive; it is a recognition that life is always unfolding as it must, even when you cannot see the bigger picture.

When you trust, you stop gripping so tightly. You realize

that you do not need to have all the answers or control every detail. Trust allows you to flow with life rather than against it, to meet each moment with openness rather than resistance. In this flow, you find a freedom that is deeper and more enduring than anything the mind can create

Reclaiming Your True Self

When you let go of the mind's chatter, the ego's attachments, and the fear of the unknown, you reconnect with your true self. This self is not defined by roles, achievements, or past experiences. It is not bound by the stories the mind tells. It is the stillness beneath the noise, the awareness that simply is.

To let go is to come home to yourself. It is to rediscover the peace, joy, and freedom that have always been within you. In this state, life no longer feels like a struggle or a problem to be solved. It feels like a gift—a dynamic, ever-unfolding mystery to be experienced with wonder and gratitude.

A Reflection

Ask yourself:

What am I still holding onto that no longer serves me?

What would it feel like to release this, to let it go with trust and acceptance?

What freedom might I discover if I stopped resisting and started flowing with life?

The Ultimate Realization

Letting go is not about losing; it is about finding. It is about finding the freedom to live fully, the courage to trust life, and the wisdom to see that you are already whole. The mind will resist this truth, insisting that you need to hold on to something—an idea, a role, a fear. But the deeper part of you knows that freedom lies in releasing, not in gripping.

As you let go, you do not diminish yourself; you expand. You do not lose your power; you reclaim it. And you do not move away from life; you step into it more fully than ever before. This is the freedom in letting go—the freedom to be, the freedom to trust, and the freedom to live as your truest self.

Trust life, let go, and discover the liberation that has been waiting for you all along.

Presence and Awareness: Lifelong Companions for Freedom

The journey of letting go, surrendering, and embracing the unknown is not a destination but a way of being—a practice to carry with you throughout life. Presence and awareness are not momentary tools; they are lifelong companions, guiding you through every challenge, joy, and uncertainty you encounter. They are your anchor in the ever-changing tides of life, offering clarity, peace, and a connection to your truest self.

To practice presence and awareness is to live intentionally. It is to meet each moment as it is, without resistance or judgment. It is to see life not as something to conquer or control but as something to experience fully, with curiosity and openness. These practices are not separate from your daily life; they are woven into every thought, every breath, and every action.

Why Practice Is Lifelong

Presence and awareness are not skills to master or goals to

achieve; they are states of being that require consistent attention. The mind, conditioned by years of habits and patterns, will often try to pull you back into old ways of thinking and reacting. Fear, attachment, and resistance may resurface, but each of these moments is an opportunity to return to awareness.

Life is dynamic, and as it changes, so will your challenges. Practicing presence ensures that you remain rooted, no matter what unfolds. It reminds you that freedom is not found in controlling life but in meeting it with openness, moment by moment.

The Beauty of Continuous Practice

Presence and awareness are not burdens to carry but gifts to embrace. Each time you pause to notice your breath, observe a thought, or feel the sensations in your body, you strengthen your connection to the now. Each moment of awareness brings you closer to the peace and freedom that are always within you.

Continuous practice does not mean striving for perfection. There will be moments when you feel disconnected, caught up in the mind's chatter, or overwhelmed by life's demands. These moments are not failures; they are reminders to return to the present. Each return is a renewal, a reaffirmation of your commitment to live fully and freely.

Practical Ways to Continue Practicing

1. Begin Each Day with Intention. Start your day by grounding yourself in presence. Take a few moments to breathe, observe, and set the intention to approach the day with awareness.

2. Pause and Reset. Throughout the day, create small

pauses to reconnect with the now. Whether you are working, walking, or engaging with others, use these moments to bring your attention back to your breath or the sensations in your body.

3. Reflect Daily. At the end of each day, take time to reflect on how you practiced presence. Ask yourself: *Where was I fully present today? Where did I get lost in thought? How can I bring more awareness to tomorrow?*

4. Embrace Challenges as Opportunities. When challenges arise, see them as opportunities to deepen your practice. Instead of reacting, pause and observe. Ask: *What is this moment teaching me?*

5. Cultivate Gratitude. Gratitude anchors you in the present moment. Regularly reflect on the beauty and abundance in your life, no matter how small or simple.

Presence as a Lifelong Companion

Presence and awareness are not practices you do—they are ways of being. They are always available to you, waiting to guide you back to the reality of now. They are your companions in joy, helping you savor life's beauty, and in sorrow, helping you navigate challenges with grace.

To live with presence is to live with freedom. It is to step out of the mind's stories and into the aliveness of each moment. It is to trust that no matter where life takes you, the present moment will always be your home.

An Invitation to the Reader

As you move forward, let presence and awareness walk beside you. Carry them into your relationships, your work, your dreams, and your challenges. Trust that they will guide you, offering clarity when life feels uncertain and peace when the world feels overwhelming.

Ask yourself:

How can I bring more presence to this moment?

What is happening now, beneath the noise of thought?

What does it feel like to simply be, here and now?

Each moment is a new beginning, a chance to return to yourself. Embrace presence and awareness as lifelong companions, and you will find that the freedom you seek is always with you, waiting to be noticed, waiting to be lived.

The Beauty of Impermanence and the Joy of Living Unburdened

Life is a dance of impermanence. Every moment, every breath, every experience arises, unfolds, and then passes away. Nothing in this world remains fixed or permanent, and while the mind often resists this truth, there is profound beauty in it. Impermanence is not something to fear; it is what gives life its vibrancy and meaning. It reminds us that nothing is stagnant, that life is always in motion, always evolving, and always offering us new opportunities to begin again.

When you embrace impermanence, you begin to see the fleeting nature of both joy and sorrow not as a loss but as a gift. Joy becomes sweeter because you know it cannot last forever. Challenges become more bearable because you know they, too, will pass. Impermanence teaches us to hold life lightly, to savor the moments we have without clinging to them, and to release them when it is time to let them go.

The Beauty of Change

The changing nature of life is what makes it beautiful.

Imagine a world where nothing changed—where every experience, every feeling, every moment was frozen in time. Such a world would lack depth, growth, and possibility. It is the ever-changing flow of life that gives it richness. The impermanence of a sunset makes it breathtaking, the fleeting bloom of a flower that makes it precious, and the transient nature of relationships that makes them meaningful.

To see the beauty of impermanence is to see the world with fresh eyes. It is to recognize that each moment is unique, never to be repeated. When you live with this awareness, you stop taking life for granted. You become more present, more grateful, and more alive.

The Joy of Living Unburdened

To live unburdened is to live in harmony with impermanence. It is to release the attachments, fears, and resistance that weigh you down and keep you from fully experiencing life. When you let go of the need to control, the fear of losing, and the clinging to what was, you create space for joy to arise naturally.

Living unburdened does not mean living without challenges. It means meeting those challenges with an open heart, unclouded by resistance. It means flowing with life rather than against it, trusting that each moment will provide what is needed and that every ending carries within it the seed of a new beginning.

There is a profound joy in realizing that you do not need to hold on so tightly. The past does not need to define you, the future does not need to frighten you, and the present moment is always enough. When you live unburdened, life feels lighter, freer, and more expansive. You become like a bird in flight, unbound by the weight of the earth, soaring in the freedom of the skies.

Impermanence as a Teacher

Impermanence is not just a truth to accept; it is a teacher to learn from. It teaches us:

To Let Go: Impermanence reminds us that clinging only creates suffering. When we accept that all things are transient, we can release them with grace.

To Be Present: Knowing that nothing lasts forever makes the present moment more precious. It calls us to fully engage with life as it is happening.

To Appreciate Life's Fragility: Impermanence makes us aware of the fragility of life, inspiring us to cherish our time, our relationships, and our experiences.

Impermanence teaches us that life is not a problem to be solved but a mystery to be lived. It shows us that the beauty of life lies not in its permanence but in its fleeting, ever-changing nature.

A Reflection for the Reader

As you close this book, take a moment to reflect:

What might change if I embraced impermanence instead of resisting it?

What would it feel like to live lightly, unburdened by the weight of clinging or control?

How can I savor the beauty of this moment, knowing

it will never come again?

A Final Invitation

Life is a series of moments, each one offering its own unique gift. Some moments will bring joy, others sorrow. Some will feel expansive, others constrictive. But all moments, without exception, are part of the flow of impermanence. When you live with this awareness, you stop resisting life and start celebrating it. You see that every moment, no matter how fleeting, is a thread in the tapestry of your existence.

Let this awareness guide you as you move forward. Let impermanence remind you to live fully, love deeply, and let go gracefully. Trust that even as life changes, the freedom of the present moment is always available to you. And in that freedom, you will discover the unshakable joy of living unburdened.

Embrace life as it is—a transient, beautiful, ever-unfolding mystery. And as you do, may you find the peace, freedom, and liberation that have always been waiting for you right here, in this moment.

Introduction

The Power of Now by Eckhart Tolle. A foundational book on presence and living in the moment.

Letting Go: The Pathway of Surrender by David R. Hawkins. Explores the practice of releasing attachments and resistance.

Chapter One: The Burden of the Past

Radical Acceptance: Embracing Your Life With the Heart of a Buddha by Tara Brach. A compassionate guide to releasing the hold of past experiences.

The Untethered Soul: The Journey Beyond Yourself by Michael A. Singer. (Examines how past patterns shape our lives and how to let go of them.)

Chapter Two: The Illusion of Control

When Things Fall Apart: Heart Advice for Difficult Times by Pema Chödrön. Focuses on navigating uncertainty and relinquishing the need to control.

Man's Search for Meaning by Viktor E. Frankl. Explores finding meaning in life's uncontrollable circumstances.

Chapter Three: The Cost of Holding On

The Book of Joy: Lasting Happiness in a Changing World by

Dalai Lama and Desmond Tutu. A reflection on how holding onto resentment and fear limits joy.

The Four Agreements: A Practical Guide to Personal Freedom by Don Miguel Ruiz. Offers practical wisdom for letting go of self-limiting beliefs and habits.

Chapter Four: Awareness is the Key

Awareness: The Perils and Opportunities of Reality by Anthony de Mello. A powerful exploration of cultivating awareness and presence.

Start Where You Are: A Guide to Compassionate Living by Pema Chödrön. Encourages mindfulness and awareness in everyday life.)

Chapter Five: The Nature of Resistance

The Wisdom of Insecurity: A Message for an Age of Anxiety by Alan Watts. A philosophical examination of how resistance creates suffering.)

Loving What Is: Four Questions That Can Change Your Life by Byron Katie. A practical method for dissolving resistance and embracing reality.)

Chapter Six: Mindfulness as a Daily Practice

Peace Is Every Step: The Path of Mindfulness in Everyday Life by Thích Nhat Hanh. A classic guide to integrating mindfulness into daily life.

Mindfulness in Plain English by Bhante Henepola Gunaratana. A straightforward introduction to mindfulness and meditation practice.

Chapter Seven: The Power of Presence

Be Here Now by Ram Dass. A profound exploration of living fully in the present moment.

Wherever You Go, There You Are: Mindfulness Meditation in Everyday Life by Jon Kabat-Zinn. A practical guide to cultivating presence in all aspects of life.

Chapter Eight: Surrender and Acceptance

The Art of Surrender: A Practical Guide to Enlightened Happiness and Well-Being by Eiman Al Zaabi. Explores the role of surrender in achieving peace and happiness.

The Gifts of Imperfection by Brené Brown. A guide to releasing perfectionism and embracing vulnerability.

Chapter Nine: Embracing the Unknown

Daring Greatly: How the Courage to Be Vulnerable Transforms the Way We Live, Love, Parent, and Lead by Brené Brown. Explores how embracing uncertainty leads to growth and authenticity.

The Way of Transition: Embracing Life's Most Difficult Moments by William Bridges. A thoughtful exploration of navigating the unknown and finding transformation in life's transitions.

Conclusion: Freedom in Letting Go

No Death, No Fear: Comforting Wisdom for Life by Thích Nhat Hanh. Examines impermanence and how it frees us to live fully.

Breaking the Habit of Being Yourself: How to Lose Your Mind and Create a New One by Dr. Joe Dispenza. Offers insights into releasing mental patterns and stepping into freedom.

Brown, Brené. *The Gifts of Imperfection: Let Go of Who You Think You're Supposed to Be and Embrace Who You Are.* Center City, MN: Hazelden Publishing, 2010.

Chödrön, Pema. *Start Where You Are: A Guide to Compassionate Living.* Boston: Shambhala Publications, 1994.

Chödrön, Pema. *When Things Fall Apart: Heart Advice for Difficult Times.* Boston: Shambhala Publications, 1997.

Chopra, Deepak. *The Seven Spiritual Laws of Success: A Practical Guide to the Fulfillment of Your Dreams.* San Rafael, CA: Amber-Allen Publishing, 1994.

Dass, Ram. *Be Here Now.* San Cristobal, NM: Lama Foundation, 1971.

De Mello, Anthony. *Awareness: The Perils and Opportunities of Reality.* New York: Image Books, 1990.

Frankl, Viktor E. *Man's Search for Meaning.* Boston: Beacon Press, 1959.

Gunaratana, Bhante Henepola. *Mindfulness in Plain English.* Boston: Wisdom Publications, 1994.

Hanh, Thich Nhat. *No Death, No Fear: Comforting Wisdom for Life.* New York: Riverhead Books, 2002.

Hanh, Thich Nhat. *Peace Is Every Step: The Path of Mindfulness in Everyday Life.* New York: Bantam Books, 1991.

Hanh, Thich Nhat. *The Heart of the Buddha's Teaching:*

Transforming Suffering into Peace, Joy, and Liberation. New York: Broadway Books, 1998.

Jakes, T.D. *Let It Go: Forgive So You Can Be Forgiven.* New York: Atria Books, 2012.

Jung, Carl. *The Collected Works of C.G. Jung: Volume 9 (Part 2): Aion: Researches into the Phenomenology of the Self.* Princeton: Princeton University Press, 1959.

Kabat-Zinn, Jon. *Wherever You Go, There You Are: Mindfulness Meditation in Everyday Life.* New York: Hachette Books, 1994.

Keller, Helen. *The Open Door.* Garden City, NY: Doubleday, 1957.

Kornfield, Jack. *The Art of Forgiveness, Lovingkindness, and Peace.* New York: Bantam Books, 2002.

Le Guin, Ursula K. *The Left Hand of Darkness.* New York: Ace Books, 1969.

Ruiz, Don Miguel. *The Four Agreements: A Practical Guide to Personal Freedom.* San Rafael, CA: Amber-Allen Publishing, 1997.

Singer, Michael A. *The Untethered Soul: The Journey Beyond Yourself.* Novato, CA: New Harbinger Publications, 2007.

Tolle, Eckhart. *A New Earth: Awakening to Your Life's Purpose.* New York: Penguin Group, 2005.

Tolle, Eckhart. *The Power of Now: A Guide to Spiritual Enlightenment.* Novato, CA: New World Library, 1997.

Watts, Alan. *The Wisdom of Insecurity: A Message for an Age of Anxiety.* New York: Vintage Books, 1951.

We'd Love to Hear From You!

Thank you so much for reading this book-it means the world to me. If you found it helpful, inspiring, or just enjoyable, would you take a moment to leave a review? Your feedback not only helps others but also keeps me motivated to create more valuable content for you.

Here's how you can leave a review:

1. Scan the QR code on this page to go directly to the Author's page.

2. Or, visit your Amazon Orders page, find this book, and click "Write a Product Review."

Your kind words make a big difference.
Thank you for your support!

www.ingramcontent.com/pod-product-compliance
Lightning Source LLC
Chambersburg PA
CBHW070833160726
48004CB00001B/362